LIVING SUCCESSFULLY WITH CHRONIC PAIN

Ruth Stella MacLean RN BCOMM

LIVING SUCCESSFULLY WITH CHRONIC PAIN

Ruth Stella MacLean RN BCOMM

Living Successfully With Chronic Pain - Copyright 2011 by Ruth Stella MacLean RN BCOMM

All rights reserved. Without limiting the rights under copyright reserved above, no part of this publication may be reproduced, stored in or introduced into a retrieval system, or transmitted, in any form, or by any means (electronic, mechanical, photocopying, recording, or otherwise) without the prior written permission of the copyright owner.

This book is licensed for your personal enjoyment only. If you would like to share this book with another person, please purchase an additional copy for each recipient. Thank you for respecting the hard work of this author.

Living Successfully with Chronic Pain offers the personal experience of the author.

This book is sold with the understanding that the author is not engaged in rendering any psychological, financial, legal or other professional services. If expert assistance or counseling is needed, the services of a professional should be sought.

Cataloguing and Publication information is available from The Canadian ISBN Service System, Library and Archives Canada.

ISBN 978-0-9878295-0-4

Website: www.livingsuccessfullywithchronicpain.com

Editor Services and Formatting for Print

provided by Patricia A. Thomas http://patthomaseditor.webs.com

*This book is dedicated
to all of you who live with chronic pain.
My wish is that one day
you too will 'dance in the rain.'*

ACKNOWLEDGEMENTS

This book began one day when my older sister, Elizabeth Calder, suggested that maybe it was time for me to think about putting my story together, to demonstrate to the world that there is life after being handed a diagnosis of chronic pain. Her faith in me was the driving force behind my determination to sit day after day at my computer, dredging up all the memories, searching my written materials for those moments that helped me find my way through chronic pain. My sister did not live to see me finish this book, but her love and caring have shaped my improved life with chronic pain, and my approach to this book.

Once in awhile, you meet someone who has a huge impact on your life. I had that experience with Dr. Mary Lynch. I had just arrived back from Elizabeth's funeral when I got a call saying I had an appointment at the Pain Management Unit in Halifax, Nova Scotia. I was feeling so miserable that I could not envision myself keeping that appointment. But I did, and it was one of the best experiences of my life. When Dr. Lynch walked in, sat down and asked me to talk to her about my pain, I knew I had found someone who would listen and understand. Since that day she has supported me through bouts of pain, hours of personal doubt and the writing of this book. I am indebted to Dr. Lynch for the wonderful insights contained in her Foreword.

The people who read this book when it was a manuscript gave me such loving feedback, such caring that I will always be in their debt. Special thanks go to Judy Good, Louise Fyffe, and Marg Dorcas for their words of wisdom and encouragement. When the time came for me to seek editorial input, I found the perfect person. Thank you Pat Thomas for applying your expert editing skills to this book, and for being the kind of friend every author needs.

And finally, to the special people in my life whom I love with all my heart, thank you for your belief in me, your patience, your support and expertise. Without you this book would never have made it into print. These special people are my husband Garry, my son, Carl and my daughter, Katie.

CONTENTS

FOREWARD... 1

INTRODUCTION... 2

1 YOU AND YOUR CHRONIC PAIN... 3

This chapter helps you identify what your pain is like, and encourages you to write a description of your pain.
By writing down what your pain means to you, and seeing its impact on your life, you can begin the process of redefining your relationship with your pain. Through writing your experiences you will learn to talk effectively about your pain to members of the healthcare community, your friends, and loved ones.

2 FINDING YOU IN THE MIDST OF YOUR CHRONIC PAIN... 17

Working on you – the person with chronic pain – is the focus of this chapter. This chapter explores the damage done to your self-esteem when chronic pain becomes the focus of your life. It also suggests ways to live with your pain by finding interests and hobbies that enhance the quality of your life.

3 WHOSE PAIN IS IT?... 34

Who you share your pain with, and how much sharing is needed is the subject of this chapter. Ideas are offered on how your chronic pain affects you and your relationship with others.

4 THE JOURNEY TO A NEW LIFE WITH CHRONIC PAIN – ACCEPTANCE... 51

This chapter offers insights into how to get past your pain and accept your new reality. It also addresses how pain can help you to learn patience in order to be more accepting of yourself and others. Learning to see pain as an agent of change in your life, rather than a foreign force out to destroy your world is discussed. Accepting your pain is moving toward accepting the new you.

5   THE JOURNEY TO A NEW YOU – ACCOMMODATION . . . 64

To accept that you have pain is not defeat, but rather an opportunity to find a new approach to your life—to take advantage of your strengths and minimize your weaknesses. This chapter looks at ways to accommodate your pain by making changes in how you live and thus reducing your pain's effects on your life and giving you a new chance to find fulfillment and happiness.

6   WHEN THE PAIN HITS – YOU CAN MANAGE IT . . . 77

This chapter describes a technique used by the author to manage a bout of pain. Also included are a few ideas on how training your mind can help to ease pain, and that sometimes you can choose to experience a bout of pain, if it means you get to enjoy a part of your life you love. And how sometimes a bout of pain is worth it.

7   WHEN ALL ELSE FAILS –TAKE TIME OUT FOR DISCOVERY . . .85

People living with chronic pain sometimes need a time out. To do that, it is necessary that the person give over his or her life to twenty-four hours of pain relief in which he or she takes meds, goes to bed, forgets about what is going on around them, and most of all focuses on themselves and getting their pain under control. Another technique explored in this chapter is how to treat your pain as you would any other part of your body. Pain is now part of you and deserves your whole-hearted acceptance and care.

8   LESSONS LEARNED OVER TIME . . . 94

This chapter deals with the long-term effects of chronic pain on your life. It stresses the importance of taking control of your care and treatment in collaboration with your health care providers. How important it is to remain open to new ideas and methods of dealing with chronic pain. This chapter addresses eight issues that need to be dealt with around chronic pain in order for the individual to maintain a satisfying life around chronic pain.

ABOUT THE AUTHOR . . . 102

FOREWORD

To live with chronic pain takes a tremendous amount of positive energy and concentration and the strategies needed do not come naturally. Coping with pain is a skill that must be learned and this volume is penned by a pro. Ruth MacLean continues to live with pain and has experienced the devastation of an incurable pain diagnosis first hand. She has risen from the ashes and is now living well with pain. Through this lens and informed by her previous experience as nurse and hospital administrator Ruth has written a guidebook for others faced with this challenge.

It is hard to believe that we can identify the code in the human genome and explore the inner reaches of outer space and yet we cannot cure pain. This is in spite of the fact that we now know more about the causes of pain then ever before. The latest figures tell us that approximately one in four people suffer with persistent pain and that the rate is going up as we get better at keeping people alive longer after injuries, operations and illnesses.

Over the past twenty years I have had the privilege of working with thousands of people who live with chronic pain and through this work I have come to appreciate the power and resilience of the human spirit. No one can do it alone. It takes determination, support and strategies. This book contains the building blocks necessary to climb back up after being knocked down by pain.

Within these pages one finds a very wise and compassionate friend. This book is essential reading for anyone who suffers from or cares about someone suffering with chronic pain.

Mary E Lynch MD FRCPC

Pain Management Unit

Queen Elizabeth II Health Sciences Centre

Halifax, Nova Scotia

INTRODUCTION

I am a writer and I live with chronic pain. Twenty years ago pain ruled my life and I was filled with fear about the future and how I would cope. I was told I could end up in a wheelchair if I didn't find a way to get past my pain. For years I searched for a book written by someone who had successfully lived with chronic pain. My search uncovered lots of books and articles on the subject of chronic pain, but none dealt with the many issues people like me, living daily with chronic pain, have to face – nor did any deal with the many concerns of my family and loved ones who do their best to support me.

I was a nurse and hospital director before chronic pain forced me, after a surgical procedure, to give up my job along with a hefty chunk of my self-esteem. Faced with the effects of chronic pain on every aspect of my life, I worked hard to find ways to alter my lifestyle in order to live around the pain in a creative and satisfying way.

Today, I live a healthy, active lifestyle – despite the physical restrictions that my clotting condition and chronic pain impose upon me.

In this book I will share how I brought about the changes that turned my unsettled life with pain into a more positive experience. As well as sharing, I invite you to use this book as a vehicle for self-discovery. My wish is that you and your loved ones take this opportunity to adopt these everyday, workable solutions for coping with your chronic pain and how it impacts your lives.

I've written this book to let you know that you're not alone with your pain. There is someone who understands your struggle, who believes in you and applauds your efforts to make your life with chronic pain a good one.

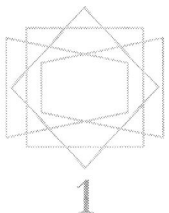

1
YOU AND YOUR CHRONIC PAIN

My pain began when I suffered extensive clotting after gallbladder surgery. The clots blocked the major veins coming back up to my heart, leaving me virtually unable to walk. I required narcotics to control the otherwise unbearable pain.

Before my surgery I was happily chasing career plans, paying more attention to my life aspirations than to the rest of me. Like most people, I simply assumed that my heart and body would go along with whatever ambitious schemes I had for my life. I viewed my surgery as a tiny bump along the road to my goals – and never considered any other result but success until a few days after the surgery when I nearly died. One of the doctors I saw in the following months told me that he didn't know how I had survived, given the extent of my clotting – a sobering message from a man in a position to know.

Those early months were mostly taken up with trying to ease the pain and cope with the feelings of loss and moments of despair, while I searched for a way to regain my ability to walk.

Hours of swimming helped me walk again, but as the months moved along, the pain didn't dissipate. I saw that I had to learn to live with my pain or withdraw from the world. To withdraw was so tempting! So much easier. All I had to do was take my pain meds and sit in front of the television. But withdrawing from life meant that I had nothing to look forward to except the next round of pain.

I couldn't live that way. Looking back on those early months, two thoughts stand out.

First, dealing with chronic pain is not only about your pain and how it behaves, it's also about how much you know about you, as a person.

Second, managing your life with chronic pain is about how much you care about yourself and how much you believe you have the right to live a happy and successful life despite your chronic pain.

Chronic pain forced me to give up my career and many of my friends, since most were work friends. Pain tore away my positive self-image, making me feel less worthy, less able to cope – someone to be pitied and looked down upon. I felt I had nothing to offer my friends from work. My feelings of inadequacy made me turn away from them. One friend persisted in being part of my life, and we are still friends because of her willingness to remain involved.

Still, I felt abandoned and alone when everyone else in my neighborhood, including my husband, went off to work. I had to make do with watching TV and wishing I had something to do other than watch the birds that moved freely in the trees outside my house.

My story isn't that much different than that of thousands of others who find their lives curtailed, their plans put on hold – possibly permanently – and who discover they have few of the skills needed to make a satisfying and productive life out of the mess created by chronic pain.

So, before going any further, I want to make something perfectly clear. Acute pain can be disruptive and difficult, but acute pain is short-term pain that will go away. When it does, life returns to the way it was for that person before the episode of pain began.

Not so with chronic pain. Having chronic pain is a long-term experience, and involves your entire body – every system in your body along with your mind and spirit. It is a life-altering endurance test that can last months or even years.

As I began to cope with my pain, I discovered that **chronic pain would test every part of me, every belief I held dear and would be a part of my life, seven days a week, fifty-two weeks of the year.**

The next big realization was that **no one could step in and take over, or take on my pain to give me a break for a while.**

Few people understood what I was trying to do when I attempted to cope with my pain. They could not imagine how it felt to suffer through pain that sapped my energy while I attempted to focus all my attention on trying to get through each painful episode.

The outside world saw me as a person with chronic pain – as someone who found it hard to smile, who might not be a pleasant person to be around, or who seemed to be preoccupied most of the time. From the perspective of someone who observed me – a family member, friend or health professional – I was a person who was hard to understand because I seemed withdrawn and sometimes agitated. **It soon became clear that those who wanted to help me were hindered by their lack of understanding, an understanding that can only come from living with chronic pain, month to month, year to year.**

I learned that chronic pain is a health issue that has consistently defied standard methods of treatment. **There is no one-size-fits-all approach that doctors can apply to treat someone with chronic pain.** For many people with chronic pain, medical management of the pain offers little in return for the hours they spend seeking a solution. Most often the search leaves the person who has the chronic pain, and the person trying to help them, in a state of frustration. It's no wonder that most people, whether health professionals, family members or friends feel helpless around someone with chronic pain.

Now that we've got those basic points out of the way, let's get on to the good news.

If you're willing to take a risk, to take a chance on you and your innate abilities to manage your life with chronic pain, your life will begin to change in ways you never thought possible.

One of the side effects of chronic pain is that it shuts you down and makes you turn in on yourself. You get so wrapped up in the grinding, everyday recurrence of pain that you forget you're a whole lot more than simply someone trying to cope with chronic pain.

By taking charge of your pain, you can start to re-discover who you are, and become reacquainted with those qualities that make you a very special person. By taking this journey of discovery that I propose, you will find the new you waiting beneath your pain.

Let's start to identify this person with chronic pain.

Often those of us with chronic pain are strong, stoic, determined, have a wry sense of humor, and are under no illusion about how difficult life can be. Though these are the qualities others see, we are much more. We have to be. Think about all the skills you need to manage your chronic pain. These skills include the ability to be patient and understanding, to work hard, and to face disappointment while searching for solutions to problems. Where else would you find such a demanding list of qualifications in a job description? And living with chronic pain is a full time job – without salary and without vacations.

Of course friends and family are sympathetic and understanding and all those other good things, but at the end of the day, it's you, and only you in charge of your situation.

I know only too well how difficult it is to be left in charge of something that affects every part of life. There seems to be so much to deal with all at once that it's difficult to know where to start. With this idea in mind, we need to look at the scope of this condition known as chronic pain.

My experience can provide a starting place. If you like, you may make notes in the margins as you read along to mark any of your experiences that mirror mine – or others that come to mind. Although the causes, locations and behaviors of your chronic pain are unique to you, I believe most of us who experience chronic pain share similarities.

At the end of each chapter you will find ideas for you to explore in relation to your pain, along with space for you to write any ideas you have about redirecting your efforts to manage your pain. Working this way helped me, and I hope it helps you as well.

As I mentioned before, the pain caused by the clotting was almost more than I could withstand. It crushed all thoughts but those that related to finding relief. The intense episodes of pain left me unable to stand or walk without experiencing excruciating pain. Nothing diminished this invasive force, not even the pain medication doctors prescribed.

Pain blocked my ability to think clearly, to articulate what I was feeling. Like a huge cloud, it blotted out my old life, making it almost impossible for me to organize the tasks needed to manage my life such as bathing, talking on the phone or sitting quietly with my family. .Something as simple as reading was nearly impossible. I couldn't concentrate because trying to control the pain took all my attention. This was all so new for me and each activity took so much energy that I could barely manage each day, let alone plan for the future.

I had to leave my job, but was optimistic that on a part-time basis I'd be able to use some of my business skills, systems management skills or nursing skills and work from home. My unrelenting pain and the hospital's inability to adapt to the concept of working from home crushed that hope.

I left my career and most of my friends behind. Most of my time was spent alone in my home. My promising life was in shambles and pain dogged every move I made. My self-image was also in tatters. Do my circumstances sound familiar?

I want to share something important with you. **In order to stem the feelings of loss coupled with anger, I needed someone who could provide me with a way out of this situation. Deep down, what I really wished for was someone who could take away this pain, and give me back my life.** You see I was stuck on the idea that one quick fix would do it. I wanted to be rescued from my pain.

I spent a lot of frustrating hours before it slowly began to dawn on me that I could take a few of the steps on my own. I could pay attention to the behavior of my pain and I try to learn more about it. If I knew more about what I was dealing with, I might be able to gain some control.

I discovered that my long bouts of pain – and I'm talking hours here – were always preceded by an incredible feeling of tiredness and lethargy. At first, I tried to fight this indicator of pain, but I soon learned that **by ignoring my body's early warning system, I spent much more time in a pain episode and the pain was more intense than if I'd given in to the tiredness and rested instead of getting tense and upset**.

As each day passed it became clear that I had to listen to my body. If I paid attention to my body, I had a chance to make a positive difference in how the pain episode progressed.

During those early months of pain I came to see that this was my pain – mine to deal with, mine to learn from – and what I learned provided a foundation from which I developed a plan for living with my pain. That realization doesn't sound like much, but it was crucial to me because without this moment of reckoning, I would have continued to wait around for someone else to fix my pain.

==After recognizing that this pain was my pain, I focused on how to live well in spite of the pain.== This was my first conscious attempt to exert control over my pain-filled life.

I wanted a life that didn't revolve around my pain. Maybe I would have to live a modified life, and maybe that life wouldn't bear much resemblance to what I had before, but I wanted a life in which I could cope with my pain and pursue a hobby – perhaps even find a job I could do from home.

But at that moment my reality was much different. I found that the inner strength required by me, a person living with chronic pain, was huge and I was tested to the limit by the obstacles that I had to overcome to make myself a new life.

One of my biggest obstacles was learning to wear heavy, ugly support stockings. They were hot, uncomfortable and sometimes painful. But without these, I would have even more pain. Another major obstacle was my inability to stand more than fifteen minutes before I developed pain. I had to give up going anywhere that involved a lineup. That meant that anything I planned to do had to be considered on the basis of whether or not I had to stand. Sitting for an hour still brings on pain, again forcing me to either skip those activities or try to modify how I manage to sit for long periods.

From this I realized that only the individual living with chronic pain can be completely aware of how complex and emotionally draining this process of rebuilding his or her life can be. And in those early months of confusion and fear, it was pretty well impossible to explain to anyone what was really going on – mostly because I didn't know! ==I could not accept that I would live this way forever==. I even denied that ==the person struggling== with pain was me!

Then, in the midst of that disheartening awareness I faced another problem. Despite the doctor's encouragement to face reality, I still hadn't thought of my pain as being chronic – here to stay…a permanent part of my life. I saw my pain as a complication that I would look after – but only until it went away. In other words, **I was looking for a way out of my chronic pain**.

I believed that medical science would come up with a remedy for my problem. I spent a great deal of time hoping that one day I would wake up and the pain would have gone.

I believed that searching for someone or something to simply take away the pain is a pretty normal way to face the situation in the beginning. We search for the quick solution – one that allows us to wait on the sidelines for the pain to be removed by someone or something outside ourselves. No wonder we want this quick exit from pain, given how confusing and difficult life can be under the circumstances.

We need to keep in mind that these thoughts of denial and quick fixes are normal, even important thoughts for all of us with chronic pain. In those early months, denial is one of the most important tools you have because it helps you get past those early disappointments, and begin your adjustment to your changed circumstances.

Those early months are all about finding a way to get through each day with chronic pain. At first I was ashamed of myself because I simply couldn't come to grips with what had happened. Why was I so determined to remain fixated on the belief that the pain and all it represented in my life would surely go away with time?

Though denial may be helpful, even necessary, one of my doctors warned me that I could not allow denial to become a permanent part of how I dealt with my pain. Some of the people I've spoken with don't ever get past this point of waiting to be rescued from the pain.

When they can't get past this point, they give up on themselves. If you're one of those, I implore you to reconsider. Start thinking about yourself, how valuable you are as a person, and begin your search for a more beneficial way to cope with your pain.

Despite my need to hide behind my denial, it eventually became obvious to me that pain had changed my life to the point where each day held less meaning for me, and I would have little to look forward to unless something changed.

I'm sure you can add a whole list of other words to describe how you feel about what happened to you and your life when the pain didn't go away. As your pain began to take over your life, did your sense of hopelessness increase like mine did?

For long days I wallowed in what seemed to be endless pain. I found myself getting angry and resentful. Like many others experiencing chronic pain, my mind was consumed with negative thoughts and emotions that seemed to make my pain worse. **My negative emotions, thoughts and feelings empowered my pain…not me.**

This realization was the first step toward coming to grips with how I might improve my ability to cope with my pain. My pain eased when I concentrated on more positive feelings. And quite frankly, the pain narcotic helped create a sense of euphoria that lifted me, at least temporarily, out of my longing for my past life – a welcome reprieve. By focusing on positive feelings I was able to alter the level of my pain – in positive ways.

But now that I had discovered this, where did I go from here? How could I get more control of this situation?

It seemed to me that being able to describe the physical shape of my chronic pain might prove very helpful. I visualized large lumps blocking the blood flow, creating pain in my legs and abdomen. I imagined how hard my body was working to clear a path past the blocked veins.

I could describe my pain in detail – as can you. You know where it is, how much of your body is involved, how it hurts, whether it comes in waves or grinds away at you. You can describe the time of day the worst pain occurs and how long it lasts, whether your pain medication helps or simply makes you drowsy and dopey. Perhaps your medication makes the pain seem worse!

You can probably also describe what I've come to call the 'after-pain,' or the pain you feel when the big pain subsides. I think of after-pain as being like the aftershock of an earthquake.

And you likely know the exhaustion that goes with that pain – how debilitating it is. I was exhausted and it was difficult for me to return to my day after the pain eased…if it eased. There are so many things we can describe about our pain – not the least of which is how many times we've given our lives over to it.

After months of flailing around, victimized by my pain, I learned something that I still apply today: **I learned that we need to write** down every word of the pain, the full description of it, in as many different ways as we possibly can. Use a dictionary or thesaurus if need be, but get the complete description of your pain on paper.

Write as much as you need to. It's your description and you're entitled to write in a way that satisfies you. If you use a computer, **be sure to print off a copy of what you've written**. This description of your pain is crucial for what we can accomplish in the chapters ahead. When you've finished, carefully read what you've written.

A friend suggested doing a daily color chart of your pain. Pick a color (red?) that represents the worst pain, and then lighter colors or shades of red to denote the lesser pain levels. Wish I'd thought of that all those years ago. What's important in all this is to look at the quality of your pain, how much pain you've survived and how long you've survived it.

To have endured what you've described makes you one hell of a person.

Don't let anyone ever suggest anything different about you, your pain and your courage. **You are a special person living in exceptional circumstances**. Look around at your friends, your family. How many of them could have lived through what you've lived through…and what you continue to live through?

You are easily one of the strongest individuals anywhere on planet Earth. You've given up so much to accommodate your pain and each one of its life-changing aspects. You've also learned to cope with the pain any way you can. Now you might consider writing about the different things you're doing to cope with your pain. Don't forget to include the impact the pain has made on your life. These notes will prove very useful to you when you meet with any of the health professionals involved in your care.

Once you've written down these coping mechanisms and the changes in your life, look at where you were during those early weeks with your chronic pain, and how much you've accomplished.

Celebrate your success. And from here on, treat yourself with the respect you deserve.

Meanwhile, I'd like you to place the written description of your pain somewhere safe so that you can find it easily and go back to it. I also invite you to take advantage of the pages at the end of each chapter to make notes on how you can apply my ideas and my experience to improve your life with chronic pain.

Before you read the second chapter, take this opportunity to focus on who you are and where you want your life to go. **Right now is the very best time to take stock of your life with chronic pain, and then to look forward and find ways you can improve your life. Make your new life the best it can be because you deserve the best life has to offer.**

Notes and Ideas

How long have you had chronic pain?

August 2012

What is the most frightening aspect of your pain?

Not being able to control neg. thoughts

Can you describe your pain? Where is it? When do you have pain? How bad is it?

Burning, throbbing, Searing, Almost daily through out day. between a 3-10

Do you take your pain meds as soon as the pain starts?

Take anti-Seizure meds daily.

Do you get relief from your pain meds?

Just a bandaid for pain!

Would you consider doing a color chart of your pain?

Already do.

Can you put together a list of things you do to cope with your pain?

Acupuncture, Cold Packs, Keep mind Busy

Are there other techniques or treatments you'd like to try?

Yes, mayo clinic may help with Learned Techniques

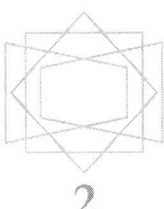

2

FINDING YOU IN THE MIDST OF YOUR CHRONIC PAIN

Remember when you discovered how many activities you could no longer do because of your level of pain? Or you discovered that you had severe restrictions on your mobility due to chronic pain? Remember how cheated and upset this made you feel?

I remember when I first realized that there were things I couldn't do because the pain would be too much, or when I came face to face with the consequences of too much physical activity – longer bouts of pain than usual. Shortly after I'd been discharged from my six-week stay in hospital, I was home and wanted to go for a walk along the pathway around my home. I made it around the path, but when I got back to the door, I had so much pain and discomfort I had to go to bed. I was so shocked and upset, I cried for hours.

And that was only the beginning of a long list of things I was to discover I couldn't do. I couldn't run, I couldn't walk or stand for any length of time. I couldn't ride my bike and I couldn't ski. Climbing stairs had become a painful experience. I couldn't lift heavy objects, or pull anything like a child's sled or push something like a lawn mower or baby stroller without pain. Imagine being afraid of the pain that lifting your grandchild would inflict?

Finding out how limited my mobility was caused me a great deal of anguish. And let me tell you, there was a good amount of swearing going on in our house – all by me. I was angry at me, at my life and the whole world. But mostly I was angered by the thought that there was little I could do to change my circumstances.

That first year – when everything I'd known about myself was now in question – set the stage for what I consider to be the most critical point in the whole chronic pain experience. Everything I'd taken for granted was either altered or ceased to exist because of the pain. I was plagued by self-doubt and overwhelmed by feelings of loss, and was virtually unable to articulate my feelings – so profound was my sense of loss.

I had never before lived with so much stress, and all of it triggered by the disappearance of the me I'd been all my life – until the chronic pain!

Who was I now? How would I ever be able to cope? Where did I fit in the world now that I didn't have my career?

Like you, I was forced by the demands of my pain to see myself, and my life in relation to my pain rather than seeing my pain as just one part of my life. Life became a daily exercise of trying to keep the pain from taking total control of my thoughts and activities.

I felt completely trapped and powerless.

In the midst of this daily struggle, I came to a frightening realization. **Looking for the right pain medication or treatment that will lessen your pain uses up a great deal of energy.**

In that search I changed from being an individual who looked forward to living my life, to a person who searched for someone outside myself who could understand my need for pain relief – someone who would be able and willing to help me.

What a hell of a place to be!

If this need for pain relief is not addressed adequately we risk losing a big chunk of who we are and what we want to be. We find ourselves talking about our pain to anyone who will listen, and worrying about what will happen if we don't get relief.

The continuous preoccupation with alleviating pain forces us to accept that not only must we find the mental resources to cope, we must also help those around us understand what we are going through when we have pain. The anxiety of trying to juggle so much at once leads us to behave in ways our family and friends don't recognize. They try to help, but sometimes their suggestions make things worse, leaving you all feeling awkward. The sense of isolation is heightened.

It is easy for us to become so impatient with the grinding inevitability of chronic pain that we let our impatience spill over to those closest to us. In seeking to explain our pain and how it makes us feel, we often find that our family, our friends and even health care providers begin to label us 'difficult.' They don't mean to label us, but when they can't experience the pain or see what is causing the pain, they feel helpless to do anything useful about it.

Yet, we keep demanding that they do help us because we need them so much. This is why it is vital to find the words to describe the pain and its impact. I know it's hard, and often it causes feelings of extreme sadness to admit that you aren't the person you were before the pain. And the truth is you're only beginning to learn about this new person and their limitations while you fight to make the adjustments demanded by your pain.

Regardless of how difficult it can be, it's important to take time to carefully explain your pain and its impact to those people who matter in your life. If not, their lack of understanding can create a barrier between you.

As the weeks move along, instead of maintaining our identity as a mother, father, librarian, nurse, lawyer, plumber or whatever our previous job was, we become someone who must endure a life with chronic pain. This label can't help but alter how people see us, and how they respond to us.

But more importantly, this change in focus alters how we see ourselves. We lose our ability to separate who we are from the pain we experience. This shift in perspective slows the process of dealing with the pain and its impact on our lives.

Okay, so what can we do?

Over the years, I have come to understand why we lose perspective and I offer you a few ideas on how to steer your self-image away from one masked by pain to an image of someone who is positive and enthusiastic about a life lived with chronic pain.

Chronic pain is just that – chronic. And at first glance alleviating it seems pretty hopeless, but there is one bright point that I think we tend to forget during all this. I know I forgot about it. And that is, **people want to help**. They've seen you, their friend or family member, suffer with pain – from whatever cause – and they want to offer what they can by way of supportive ideas. Each of us knows how much worse off we'd be if we didn't have these people in our lives. So we need to take time to appreciate them for what they offer and let them be a part of what is going on with us when we can.

But we need to remember we're working with a concerned friend or a health professional who cannot see or feel our pain. We try to explain our pain – something that is so crystal clear to us – in words that can't begin to describe what is happening in our bodies. Because our pain is chronic, it feels as if we're constantly in situations that require that we explain how our pain feels, and why we can no longer do some things that used to be a normal part of our lives – before the pain.

Imagine trying to explain what Beethoven's 5th Symphony sounds like to someone who can't hear?

How would we explain moonlight to someone who can't see?

How do we explain chronic pain to someone who has never experienced such pain?

This dilemma is the root of the problem when it comes to getting help with our pain issues. In order to regain control of our lives, we need to get control of our pain. Getting control of our pain means getting a healthcare professional to understand that we are willing to work with them to find adequate pain relief.

Unfortunately, we often can't give a clear picture of the pain going on in our bodies, except to point out the location and hope that we are understood. Like me, I'm sure you've been asked by a very caring health professional to 'rate' the intensity of your pain. A rating is a comparison so the question is, 'compared to what?' What do you use as a standard or as a frame of reference? To give it a rating from 1-10 would be funny, if it weren't so critical for how the various health professionals respond to your situation.

If you have a rash or a broken bone, or any visible physical complaint, it's so much easier for you and the health professional to come up with a solution. You have visible proof of the problem. You can point to a part of your body and show where the problem is and clarify how it affects you. Having a visible or measurable cause of your pain allows you to engage in a meaningful discussion with a health professional and find a workable solution.

But when you try to describe pain that has no lesion or scar to back up your claim, it's harder to convince people your pain exists. Although they want to fix what's wrong, they cannot see what is causing the problem and must rely on what you tell them. Even the diagnostic capability of an MRI often cannot pinpoint the pain 'lesion' or originating site. It all comes down to how well you – the person with the pain – can provide words that describe your pain. These words need to persuade and must make sense to the people around you who are trying to offer solutions that could alleviate your pain.

The gap – between what you are feeling and what you're able to get people to understand you're feeling – is a major obstacle separating you from the rest of the world. By this I mean that very often, because we look 'normal,' people assume we aren't in pain. Little do they realize that looking normal takes a lot of energy. **Facing the world when you're struggling with pain is a major feat of endurance.**

Your challenge is to use the notes you've written in the first chapter, and your recognition of the impact of your pain on your life, to encourage and support your doctor to help you. **Your continued efforts to communicate will provide your doctor with essential information.**

We'll come back to this, but in the meantime, it's important to recognize something else. **This is the time to start putting together a team of professionals who offer you good care, and who understand you and your issues around pain. It may take time to find the right doctor, physiotherapist or massage therapist, but one of your responsibilities to yourself is to keep searching until you find these people.**

This search for the right support and help is often tedious and very slow – and sometimes it's quite discouraging. The sense of frustration as you search to find the health professionals who understand your situation and are willing to help often leads to negative feelings that, if unchecked, can spill over into other aspects of your life.

Added to this is the sense of powerlessness that can be part of the frustration you experience, not only in seeking the right health professionals but also in managing your day-to-day life. I'm sure you've faced many situations where your pain prevented you from doing something and you turned down a chance to take part in an activity you love. And it seems to happen so frequently that you, and the person offering you the opportunity, feel frustrated that your pain has once again interfered. We can all list ways in which our chronic pain results in these kinds of negative feelings.

Through time I discovered something that is key to managing my pain.

You cannot continue to be defined by the negative side of your pain experience as it is demoralizing and can lead to a great deal of disappointment and unhappiness.

This continued interference in your life brought on by your chronic pain will eventually lead you to face the decision: do you want to be defined by who you are as a person with chronic pain or do you want to be seen not only as a person who lives with chronic pain, but also as one who manages to have a job, or pursues an interest, or has a hobby that provides a non-pain related identity?

In other words, you are more than simply a person with chronic pain.

As I write that statement I am so aware of how hard it was for me to come to that realization. But when I finally did, I was able to give some thought to what I could do differently.

Number one on my list was adequate control of my pain.

Pain is extremely exhausting. And it's been my experience that if pain isn't reasonably well managed it will bring on more pain. This pain-triggering-pain cycle can become a very destructive force in your life. It might take months or even years to organize your pain control techniques, but you must find the pain control that works for you.

For some reason – like so many other people with chronic pain – I was determined not to take the pain meds as ordered by my doctor. I believed that the narcotic I was prescribed should be an optional last resort.

Here's the lesson I finally learned. **Don't think you can 'tough it out' when it comes to your pain.** Seeking pain control when the pain starts, or when your body gives you a warning sign, is not an indication of weakness, but rather an essential part of a smart person's plan to live comfortably with pain. You must find the best pain treatment that fits your need for pain control, keeping in mind that it is unlikely that even with the appropriate amount of pain medication you will be completely pain free. Reaching the best level of pain management can include a combination of pain medications, meditation techniques, or a complete change in how you organize your daily activities.

For instance, in my case, I had to find a way to keep my legs elevated as much of the time as possible to relieve as much of the pain as possible. It took practice to always remember to search for a chair in a restaurant where I could put my feet up on another chair close by. I soon preferred restaurants with booths or tablecloths so that no one would notice when I edged my feet up onto the seat of another chair or the bench across from me. I found that most pain medications weren't really effective in managing pain. They needed to be combined with other forms of treatment or activities to give me the best pain relief

Through trial and error in the early years, I discovered I was more likely to gain relief from baths and relaxation techniques combined with pain medication. But these methods required a huge time commitment, and sometimes they didn't work well at all. Sometimes I would spend hours in pain during which nothing worked. On those occasions I simply did what I could and waited for the pain to ease.

I also learned not to let people who have never gone through what you're going through, decide whether or not you have pain or tell you how intense it is. We often wish we could accept what they say as the facts of the situation, even though we know we have pain. But it's essential that you remain true to yourself by quietly acknowledging that people who don't have pain are not in a position to make a judgment about your pain.

And **chronic pain often makes it difficult, if not impossible, to step back and look at what is going on – to gain a different perspective on the problem. One of the best techniques I've found over the years to get a perspective on my pain is to keep a personal journal.** Such a journal is in addition to the pain description I talked about earlier.

I use my journal as a private place to put down my thoughts and feelings, but also to describe what my life was like during those years, to see my progress. Writing about my pain proved to be a very useful exercise that helped me in two very important areas of my life.

First, **keeping a written journal of my pain** – when it occurred, how long it lasted, what made it worse or better – **was very helpful in talking to health professionals about the best way to proceed with my treatment.**

Second, **by writing down my thoughts and feelings, I was able to better understand what was happening to me,** and to see, as I mentioned before, just how big a role my emotional state played in the level and duration of my pain.

Writing about my feelings allowed me to see how much my life had changed and to discover what mattered most to me in my changed circumstances. But I didn't share everything I wrote – I kept part of my journal hidden. Why? Because some of the thoughts and issues I wrote about could worry others if they accidentally come across them. And because I needed a safe place to vent my worst worries and concerns without fear of someone reading them.

By reading over what I'd written I was able to see that I could use what I knew to change my self-image from that of a person with chronic pain to one with a hobby or special interest, and to have a focus in my life other than my pain. Writing these issues down provided me with an opportunity to honestly look at what I was doing about my feelings, my hopes and how it all impacted on my pain.

It led me to realize that I had it in me to concentrate on what was possible for me in my changed situation, rather than what wasn't.

I also discovered through my journal that my identity was very closely linked to my self-image, especially since so much of the physical activities I once enjoyed were no longer possible.

Along this road of developing a positive self-image, there is one major requirement, and I'm going to share it. **You may have to alter your lifestyle to live better with your chronic pain.**

Once you realize that your pain has become chronic, you can do something very positive for yourself. **By being open to change you can decide to move on to ways of spending your days in the most affirmative and personally rewarding way you can.** This process of adjusting your life in order to live better with chronic pain I've labeled 'accommodation,' and it's dealt with at length later in the book.

Redesigning my life meant that I made a list of what I could do physically, and that included the sort of activities I could do in relation to a hobby or personal interest.

Throughout the years I've lived with chronic pain, there have been several times when life would suddenly demonstrate its infinite ability to surprise me. One example comes easily to mind.

I had spent months trying to figure out what I could do with my time that would be personally fulfilling, when one day I was reminded of my dream to one day have the time to write.

Hadn't my pain presented me with the chance to be home in a quiet environment with a computer and time to learn about writing techniques, markets, and decide what type of writing I wanted to do? Writing fit in perfectly with my physical limitations; I could write sitting with my feet up, or lying down.

I would never have imagined that something as devastating as chronic pain could lead me to pursue my dream of writing.

What I'm saying here is that it is never too late to sit down and think about what you can do to make your pain-altered life more rewarding. This may require that you move away from your past skills and develop new ones.

As part of this exercise of self-discovery, take every opportunity you can to enjoy your daily life. Some people on this search for enjoyment or fulfillment say 'you should live in the moment,' and I've found this to be true. But **sometimes daydreaming in the moment is every bit as effective. Daydreaming about the little things you can change to make your life better is a great way to come up with tiny goals. Tiny goals lead to bigger ones.**

To reinforce this idea, I keep signs posted in my office space. Several of my favorite ones over the years have been: 'Smile!' 'Dream big.'

'Make plans.' 'Think positive.' 'Enjoy the process.' 'Smell the roses.' 'When life gives you lemons, make lemonade.'

Talking about space, pain often restricts physical activity so your living space needs to be as pleasant and as appealing as possible. What does that mean for you? Put some of your ideas for a more pleasant living space down on paper and see what you discover. Then translate your ideas into results. Something as simple as painting a room in a bright color can be very uplifting. And the big benefit of this exercise is that those wanting to help can do so by painting and fixing up your space.

Changing your physical space brings me to another important point. Public Image.

In my experience, **if you want to find your place in your new life, you need to decide what sort of image you want to present to the public.** As we've talked before, pain alters not only how you see yourself, but also how others see you. And a positive self-image is also about easing the sense of loss inflicted by your changed circumstances. Very often this altered image is more about you, the person suffering with chronic pain, than you the person who is making a life despite your chronic pain.

Therefore, it is so important for you to be clear in your mind about how you want to appear to others, because how they see you will influence what they think of you, and how they will respond to you. **How others see you has been altered because you've had to change in order to deal with your situation. But you're the only one who can influence how big that change will be – and in what direction.**

In the early months of my pain, I spent most of my days in sweats and T-shirts, the kind of clothes that allowed me a great degree of comfort, but were not very attractive. One day when I got up and put on my ugly elastic stockings, I decided to wear a good pair of dress pants, and a bright blue top. When I looked in the mirror, I not only looked better, I looked more like the old me. From that day on I picked days when I would dress up, and some of those days I wasn't going anywhere, just hanging around the house. But I felt so much better, so much more attractive, more like the old me.

Encouraged by this, I decided to write in my journal, and an old saying came to mind. I believe it was something an aunt of mine once said **'When you feel like a dime, dress like a million. It'll make you feel better.'**

In other words, sometimes something as simple as dressing up will make us feel good about ourselves.

In addition to our physical appearance, we need to consider how our mental state influences our thoughts. **If you feel down and out about your pain, or if you feel resentful or depressed about what the pain has done to your life, it will be reflected in how you are seen by others.** It's hard to look and sound upbeat if you're down in the dumps about how hard it is to control your pain, or how difficult it is to find time for exercise or the treatments so necessary to improve your condition.

I'm not trying to suggest that every time you see people outside your home, and immediate family, you have to put on a show of bravado or pretend that your life is perfect. Such behavior might work in the short term, but in the long run you cannot maintain this false public persona. It is too exhausting.

What I am suggesting is that you stand tall, square your shoulders, let a smile relax your face, and you will instantly feel better – take a tiny step toward feeling a whole lot better.

While I was practicing what I call 'window dressing,' I needed to figure out who this person with chronic pain really was, how I wanted my life to be and what strategies I was willing and able to work on to make living with chronic pain a more positive experience.

Like so many of you with chronic pain, I am a very capable, brave individual. That realization led me to rethink how I would meet my need to develop a better life with chronic pain.

My choices now and in the future would be based on my needs and changed circumstances. I would focus on meeting those needs.

To make good choices you need to take time out for yourself as often as possible while you work on changing how you live your life.

You may find the following list of considerations helpful, and I'm sure you'll have others to include.

>**What you need in your life to be physically comfortable.**
>
>**What your physical space needs are.**
>
>**What your need for restorative time is: how much and when.**
>
>**What your needs are to improve your emotional and physical care.**

As you write your list, the most important point to remember is to include whatever you need to feel better about yourself. This is about you and what you need.

While you work on how to accept what has happened, you can begin to make accommodations in your everyday life to make room for your chronic pain that will still leave space for you to be the person you are.

Your list can be as detailed or as short as you like. It's not the length or details of the list that's important. The important consideration is what you believe this list will accomplish for you.

Your life and how you live it is in your hands. You're in charge of what happens next.

Notes and Ideas

What would you change in your physical space if you had the opportunity?

How have your relationships with people outside your immediate family changed?

Would you be willing to keep a pain journal for a few months?

What special hobby or interest would you like to pursue if you could manage to do it?

What would you like to do to improve your self-image?

Who among your family and friends could be your advocate if you decide to make a change or to talk to your doctor about trying something new to help you manage your pain?

How comfortable are you with asking for help? If you aren't comfortable asking for help, why do you think that is? What could you change to make it easier to ask for help?

3
WHOSE PAIN IS IT?

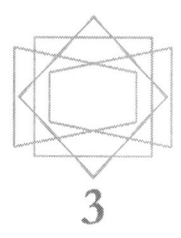

Okay, before you jump all over me for asking you this question, let me pose another question to you. How many times have you been in the presence of a member of your family, a friend or a health professional and had to listen politely while they tried to express what they 'think' your pain is, or what must be causing it?

I'm not suggesting for a moment that those who pose questions of this nature are in any way insincere or uncaring. As I said back in the first chapter, they quite frankly don't know – unless they've been where you are. They don't know how your pain feels, how intense or frightening it is, nor do they have any inkling of how it feels to have the kind of pain that leaves you exhausted and discouraged. And they cannot for a moment imagine how it must feel to face this pain and its consequences on a daily basis.

In other words, they don't know what is going on inside you and with your pain.

They only know what they can see, what you tell them and what they've learned from reading or talking with others. They can't know your pain.

This leaves you to decide how to manage your chronic pain. There's no one else but you. And that's not necessarily a bad thing.

My most memorable moment in taking charge of my pain happened when I realized I was gaining weight – a very bad development for someone whose circulation was already stressed. So, what caused my weight gain?

The answer was simple. I wasn't exercising very much. I was using my pain as an excuse to sit around. Besides, I didn't want to watch my weight. I didn't need anything more to worry about. But when I really thought about the weight issue, I realized that I could probably lessen my pain and help my circulation by setting a moderate goal weight, one I could achieve.

I lost ten pounds – a small step, but one that gave me an opportunity to take charge and to feel in control. If you find a similar opportunity, take it. You'll feel better about you and your chronic pain.

Next, I'd like to introduce a few ideas that worked for me, and that might help you find a way to regain control of your life with chronic pain.

You are in full possession of your pain. No one else has that responsibility.

Each of us with chronic pain has to find a way through our pain to a better life.

No one can make this journey for us.

Let us start with the first point, which is the ownership issue. **For better or worse, you're the only one who can make a real difference in how your pain behaves. To do this, you must communicate how you feel in order to get the help and support you need. You must act as the ears, eyes and sensory expert for those who are trying to help you.**

You have to learn to tell others what is going on with your pain, and, as I said earlier, you have to find the words for something that is almost entirely invisible to the person with whom you're trying to communicate.

Your biggest need is to become a good communicator.

And was this ever hard for me! As a nurse and therefore a caregiver, I was accustomed to being the provider of care – not the recipient. The words needed to communicate my pain did not come easily. In addition to that, I tended to think and talk in short bursts of very abbreviated sentences, assuming that the listeners understood. Wrong! **I had to relearn how to explain things to people when it came to talking about my issues around pain.** That was the steepest learning curve of my life.

Let's go back and revisit the description of your pain that you wrote as an exercise in the first chapter. What you've described there is probably far too familiar to you at the moment, but I want you to read through it and look for some very specific traits of your pain:

   time of day;

   number of times a day you have pain;

   the intensity of your pain, based on your own pain scale;

   the specific location of your pain; and

   how it affects your everyday life.

Your written pain description will be a huge help to you, and your most valuable tool in tracking your pain – and explaining your pain to your doctor or other healthcare professional. This may be an opportunity for a family member to be your advocate at the doctor's appointment by discussing what is going on in a more focused, reasoned way because they are not in pain. And because they care, they may be better able to explain the impact of your pain on your daily life that allows the doctor or health professional to suggest solutions to at least some of the issues you have around your chronic pain.

In order for there to be an effective partnership between you and those trying to help you, it is essential that you be as clear, as complete and as concise as you can be when you explain what your pain is like, how it behaves and what it's doing to you – and specifically how your pain impacts your daily living.

So why is understanding the impact of chronic pain on your daily life so critically important to you?

This sounds like a dumb question, but it's very important that you have the answer. Besides the daily pain, what else has changed in your life? What has your pain done to your life that you need help with? What would you like to change to make your life better now that you have chronic pain? What activities have you had to curtail? Very often the health professional cannot really understand your pain, or your description of your pain, but they can and do relate to how pain has changed your life.

The health professional can offer suggestions or give you access to other services that will assist you to find solutions to some of the new everyday problems in your life. For instance, if your biggest issue is mobility, your doctor can help you find the right physiotherapist or occupational therapist or offer suggestions relating to other therapies that might help.

If you don't ask you'll never know what help there is out there for you. **Be your own best advocate by talking to your doctor about what you really need to make your life better.**

Granted, what they offer may not change your pain, but their suggestions can be helpful in other ways.

For example, their support in gaining strength and mobility may make your life much easier, allowing you to **take possession of your pain and the implications of making choices on how to live your new life. It's your pain, and it's up to you to decide how best to manage your pain.**

And now I'd like to talk about an entirely different issue relating to ownership of your pain. Chronic pain requires that you decide which people you will let in on your pain and what your pain is doing to your life. And before you think I've lost it or taken too many pain meds, let me say that not everyone should be allowed into your world of pain and here are a couple of reasons why.

Some people only want the gory details of how much you suffer so they can convey the 'awful story' of your pain to others. They are essentially voyeurs, snooping around your life. You don't need to be the subject of idle, meaningless gossip by people who really don't have any role in your life with chronic pain.

Another important point is **that the more you talk about your pain, the more it's on your mind, the greater the chance that it will dig its way deeper into your life and drain more of your mental and emotional energy. You are what you think, meaning that if you think about your pain all the time, it will become the major focus of your life.**

So, who really needs to hear about your pain?

The health professionals you work with, and your loved ones who live with you are the ones who deserve your confidence and attention. I'd like to talk about them for a moment.

The health professionals involved in treating our pain are paid professionals we see on a periodic basis. They listen to what we have to say, intending to resolve at least some of our pain issues. It is very important that we learn to communicate with them as willing partners, not as adversaries.

To make this point, I'd like to tell you a story about what happened to me.

When I first started trying to live with this pain of mine, I felt a need to describe it in detail every time I visited with my doctor. I wanted to nail it all down, give every detail and make absolutely sure that the poor doctor understood how I was living my drastically altered life.

It wasn't until I had the opportunity to watch the doctor's response that it became clear that he wasn't listening. And you know why he wasn't? I was talking all around my pain, saying things about how 'it' really hurt, and basically giving him my emotional diatribe about what was happening to my life. And let me be completely honest, I was still angry about having to learn to live with chronic pain, and I needed someone to blame.

I had every right to feel this horrible sense of loss and anger. But the doctor couldn't feel anything I was talking about. He needed a specific description of my pain to guide his treatment of me. He also needed validation…to know if I'd actually done what he'd suggested at the last visit, or at least tried to do it, and whether or not my attempt was successful.

But my head wasn't there at all. I didn't want to hear what he 'thought' I should do. I wanted a real live answer to the problem, in living Technicolor with the solutions and steps spelled out in big bold letters. I did not want to spend the time and energy describing my pain in terms he could relate to. I lived with it every day and felt he should be able to 'see' what it was doing to me. More importantly, I did not want to hear that this was a chronic situation. I wanted out of this life I'd been forced into. I wanted my world back the way it was before the pain started.

It wasn't until this overworked man offered me two choices – find a way to lessen the effects of my pain, or end up in a wheelchair – that I began to take stock of what was likely to happen to me in the years ahead.

Talk about a wake-up call! And what a brave doctor he was to say what needed to be said to a woman who was itching to tell him what she thought of his advice!

In the end, I didn't tell him anything that day or any other day. What I did do was go home and begin the process of fixing my life. And one of the major fixes was that **I had to learn who needed to know about my pain, how much they needed to know and how often they needed to hear about it.**

This brings me to the flipside of pain ownership. As the person who owns your pain, you not only have to make decisions on who you'll share your pain with, but you also have to decide how much you want to share your pain with those around you, and especially those who love you most.

Here's what I've concluded in the twenty-plus years of my chronic pain.

You cannot burden those you love with each and every episode of your pain. That's right. They are not part of your pain. They are innocent bystanders.

In my life, I've been lucky to have my husband as my 'pain associate.' That is, he has been around for all of it, from the beginning. He's spent many nights awake while I tried to get my pain to settle down. He's gone to doctors' appointments and listened to me try to work out the best way to do something. A big chunk of his life has been spent standing by, encouraging me and doing those things I can no longer do.

But most helpful of all, he has come to realize that he cannot experience what I'm going through. Not any easy place to be for anyone, especially someone who loves you and wants to share your life.

But for all his caring and concern, I **would never tell him about every pain episode** I experience. I realize that sometimes this approach leaves him feeling left out and you may wonder why I sometimes don't tell him.

For the same reason that you would try to protect someone you love from unhappy news. And added to that, is **if a relationship is to be healthy, you cannot expect the person who loves you to always be there for you.**

Yeah, I know. This is not what you wanted to hear. But remember that this person who loves you also has to maintain their life around your situation. If your pain is always at the top of the agenda, how does the person you love and care about ever have a day that they don't feel guilty about how lucky they are to not have your pain?

Give the person you love the perfect gift. Some time away from your pain.

Again, it comes back to knowing who can truly feel and understand your pain – and that's you. **This pain is your problem and it's here to stay.**

Have I made you upset by saying this? Do you feel that if you can't talk about your pain to those who really care about you, then who can you talk to? Perhaps you feel that your pain is something you can't manage alone; it's too much.

I understand what you're saying and a whole lot more. But try thinking of it this way. Since the day you became aware that the rest of your life would include chronic pain, you've had no choice but to devote a great deal of time to searching for ways to live with this all-encompassing problem. You've had to be very self-absorbed in order to get your life back on track and to make it as comfortable as you could with your chronic pain. Your life was about your pain in the beginning, and rightfully so.

But your loved ones aren't suffering the pain. They are simply there with you, sharing your life, trying to cope with what it's done to you and their relationship with you. They probably still miss the old you, the one without pain.

The consequences of your pain, for them, can be very serious and life changing as well. First, they had no choice but to watch you, someone they love, go through pain they didn't understand, pain that changed you into someone they have trouble recognizing. And they feel guilty about their feelings of loss and disconnection. They feel inadequate when you're in pain. All they can do is wait to see how long the bout of pain will last.

Imagine how you'd feel if you were in their shoes.

As I've said before, this pain journey has many twists and turns, and many special moments. The moment when you realize that you own your pain, that you can decide who needs to know about your pain and how much they need to know, will be a turning point in your journey to a rewarding life with chronic pain. Seize that moment to make your decision – when your pain seems like it's about to start or get worse, do the most loving and caring thing you can do for those who love you.

Unless you need their involvement for some reason, or it's an especially acute wave of pain, do your level best to say as little and show as little of what you're going through as you possibly can. Whenever you can, spare them having to suffer with you. To do this, you may have to call a time out from your family, and go to another part of the house, or lay down quietly somewhere while you marshal your strength to ease your pain. Whatever you do to ease your pain, do it quietly and with love for them.

That's not to suggest that there won't be times when you need to involve your loved ones in your pain. But as your chronic pain continues, you will discover where and under what circumstances your family members must be brought into your very intimate, private world.

Now to the second point I made in the beginning of this chapter. Each of us who live with chronic pain has to find a way through that pain to a better life. From my experience, creating a good life with chronic pain requires a willingness to try different treatment ideas and to be open to change. I succeeded by simply working at it and by believing that a life lived successfully with chronic pain was achievable.

How many people with chronic pain manage to revamp their lives and make room for the existence of their pain?

I don't have a definitive answer. The statistics suggest that one-in-five adults in North America suffers from chronic pain – pain lasting several months or longer. This means we're definitely not alone. But there is reason to believe that many people do not get their pain under control, and **the search for pain control often stops these people from moving on with the other changes they need to make in order to live a better life.**

I've said this before – but it's worth repeating it here – **each of us must come to grips with how much pain we can tolerate, keeping in mind that we will continue to have episodes of pain that will be helped, but not necessarily eliminated, by the use of pain medication.**

Years of experience with chronic pain have shown me that there's a whole lot more to pain than simply finding an effective medication. Yes, we have pain, but for a person with chronic pain our pain is part of a bigger puzzle. There is no doubt in my mind that my pain is worse when any or several of the following things happen:

If I'm emotionally upset by something going on in my life, my pain will be more intense.

If I'm tensed up and anxious, I can actually bring on my pain! I didn't believe that at first, but as the years rolled on, I experienced this repeatedly.

Feeling tired, not getting enough rest, will set the stage for a bout of pain, and then make that pain worse!

Also, many times events in your life outside your control can add stress to your life. And stress will aggravate pain.

All the things I've listed above have two elements in common.

They are controllable behaviors, for the most part, and these behaviors are the result of us not taking care of our pain…and us.

Here's something I discovered some time ago, and it's a thought I repeat to myself frequently. **Pay attention to your pain and how it behaves in different circumstances. Then work to remove as many of the pain triggers in your life as possible.**

If you're going to get this situation under your control, and move on to make a new life for yourself, you need to work toward finding new daily patterns that consciously exclude the destructive ones that trigger your pain episodes. **You must put together a pattern for daily living that fits your need for pain control, while you discover what activities enhance your physical capabilities now altered by your pain.**

I'm a huge fan of 'Things To Do' lists because they help you plan for success. Keep in mind that most of what I'm about to say here will be dealt with in greater depth later in the book. For now, while you continue to read, here are a few points to consider as part of your positive action plan.

Pain is exhausting, so get all the rest you need. That may include naps, or eight hours at night, but whatever it is, establish a pattern that provides enough rest.

Pain can also affect your general health, and you may be more susceptible to the usual cold and flu illnesses. Make a healthy diet an absolute necessity in your new lifestyle.

Go to your family doctor for at least a yearly checkup. I realize that in the early stages of chronic pain, you feel as if you live in your doctor's office, and I empathize with your desire not to add another trip. But keeping your body healthy and free from disease is the best way to stop any further health upset that could cause havoc in your present situation.

Drop the negative feelings off at the nearest dumpster. Negative feelings are, in my opinion, the single biggest barrier to real, positive change in your life.

Find your form of meditation or spiritual renewal – and you can define this any way you choose. What's important here is to find time to be silent and alone with yourself and whatever higher force you believe in.

I am a very linear thinker and am fiercely independent, so I had a hard time with this last point. It wasn't until my sister died of a brain tumor that I began to see that there is something revitalizing and renewing when you search your heart, while listening to the stillness within.

After years of physical pain, and then the emotional pain of losing the sister I loved more than life itself, I can tell you unequivocally that life is about listening to that inner voice – whether you call it a higher being, or simply the core of who you are. It is the force that will lead you toward your new life that includes your acceptance of pain and your need for happiness.

Now, back to another point I made in the beginning of the chapter – **no one can make this journey for you. As a lifelong friend of mine put it, 'If it is to be, it is up to me.'**

How I wish that weren't true. For years I searched for the reason why I was forced into a life with chronic pain. Why me? What had I done to deserve this? I lived by the rules, did the right thing. I became a nurse to help others and here I ended up needing other people's help.

Where was the fairness in that?

Now I have a confession to make. Buried deep in my journals is a list of people I'd like to give my pain to, people who deserve it much more than I do. People who don't play by the rules, who are hurtful and uncaring. Yeah, I'm showing my nasty side, but I'm entitled. I'm living with chronic pain. We live in a world populated by feelings that may not seem correct or right to some people, but we don't have to change how we feel for anyone but ourselves. Someday I'll forget about wishing bad things on bad people…someday.

In the meantime, I remember a comment I heard a long time ago, and unfortunately I don't know who said it first, but it has become a bit of a motto of mine. 'Nothing's so bad that it can't get worse.'

Frightening, but true. So what does that mean for you? Or me? Can it get worse?

Yes. And we've already been dealt a blow to our physical well being, to our way of life and who we are. But if we don't take responsibility for our lives and for the way we live with our pain, there is no guarantee that things won't get worse. Most likely they will. Or remain unchanged and out of our control. Consuming us.

And I'm sure each of you agrees that having pain isn't the absolute worst thing that could happen in your life.

With my years of living with chronic pain, I can tell you with complete certainty that we can take what life has dealt us and make the best of it, or we can spend all our energy wishing and hoping for what will never be. I've learned that it is this present moment you're living through that matters. I believe that how you handle this and every moment in the future will determine how well you'll do over time.

Either way, it's your choice.

As I told you earlier, if you have chronic pain, you are a very special person. Because you are living with it, you also have it in you to choose behaviors that will make your life with chronic pain a better one.

Our journey to a good life with chronic pain is the subject of the next two chapters.

Notes and Ideas

Can you think of a change, big or small, that you'd like to make to give yourself a feeling of having more control in your life?

Which issues in your life with pain give you the most difficulty? How would you like to change your situation to address these issues?

Who do you feel needs to know about your pain?

Are you comfortable with talking about your pain to those who need to know?

Do you believe you have a healthy diet? If not, have you considered getting an appointment with a dietitian?

List four foods you eat that you believe are not really healthy.

Circle the one you'd be willing to give up for four weeks.

4

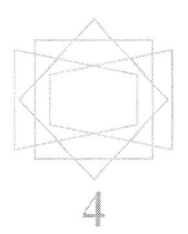

THE JOURNEY TO A NEW LIFE WITH CHRONIC PAIN – ACCEPTANCE

While visiting a friend I hadn't seen for years we talked about our lives, our children and our grandchildren. My friend said, 'I don't know how you did it, leaving a job you loved and a promising career, only to find yourself at home alone trying to deal with constant pain while your friends and family continued to be out there in the world doing what they wanted to do. And, even now, the fact that there are so many things you can't do without having pain must be discouraging. Yet, you seem to be doing so well.'

What she didn't realize was that getting from where she described my life in the beginning to where I am now took me twenty years of writing, research and effort! None of the changes – the acceptance, or the accommodation – happened easily or suddenly. At first I was discouraged and depressed by my friend's words, until I realized that what an outsider had seen as difficult – almost insurmountable – had become a way of life for me.

My life today is very different from my old life, but in many ways it is better. Hard to believe that, isn't it? Yet, not only is it true for me, it can be true for you – with just a little soul-searching and what I call an 'attitudectomy.' I invented this word when I realized that so much of what I thought and how I behaved toward my pain had to be adjusted in order for me to move forward.

The key is that as well as working on a change in attitude, you also must remove all those built-in mindsets that can block people like you and me from looking beyond our current status and pain to see a new path for our lives.

And you need to know that even after all these years, I'm still working on *me*. And if you think about it, if I had been working on becoming a brain surgeon, a concert pianist or an astronaut I would be one by now. Instead I'm still working on accepting and living with my chronic pain....

Sounds a little dismal – and if you look on the dark side, it is.

But here's the secret to living with chronic pain. If you insist on seeing only the dark side of your pain and the negative things it's done to your life, you may never be able to accept your chronic pain.

If you don't find a way to accept your chronic pain, the pain and your lack of control over your life will lead to years of unhappiness and feeling like a victim. Overwhelming feelings of bitterness will cloud your life. Trying to live your life surrounded by negative feelings and emotions is not healthy for anyone…especially for someone with chronic pain.

So, what's involved in accepting your chronic pain?

Acceptance and accommodation. These are two of the most important challenges facing a person with chronic pain.

Accommodation is about altering the mechanics of living your life in the presence of chronic pain, of making the necessary changes to your living space and the way you live in your everyday life. You can accommodate your pain without really accepting it, but it is easier if you work on accepting your pain while you accommodate it. Accommodation will be dealt with in the fifth chapter.

Acceptance means coming to terms with your situation – emotionally and mentally. And it's hard! We want to be free of pain. We want to spend our time doing pleasant things, not thinking about how our actions will be limited by our pain.

Acceptance is being open to the reality of what is – not thinking of the chronic pain as some ugly, destructive force over which you have no control. Rather it is accepting your pain as a part of who you are.

Acceptance allows you to be at ease with your pain so that you can make the necessary accommodations and move on to the greater opportunities awaiting you in your life.

Yes, the day I realized that my pain was here for the rest of my life was one of the most devastating days anyone could ever imagine, and you, another person with chronic pain, know what I mean. I felt trapped between my old expectations, wants and needs, and the new reality of my life.

But there was the key – old life versus new life.

Yes, I had a promising career, and it was true that so many activities I'd enjoyed were now denied me, but that didn't mean my life and my chance for happiness were over. It meant I had to rethink who I was and what I wanted and find what I could do to get what I wanted.

Now, acceptance didn't happen in a single moment, or at a particular time of a certain day. Acceptance happened with the slow spiritual shift from believing my life was over, to seeing a new set of possibilities. Acceptance isn't a tangible thing, but rather it's an internal shift in how we see the world. For instance, my underlying beliefs hadn't changed. I was still the same person, but faced with changes that altered how I took part in the world around me.

One thing I'd forgotten or ignored in my altered lifestyle was that lots of people for lots of different reasons, not just people with chronic pain, discover that their lives have been permanently changed at some point in their lives. That does not mean they withdraw from their lives, but rather they adjust, regroup and discover what else might be out there for them.

My life with pain required a change in mindset, an emotional discovery about who I was and what really mattered. My very busy life before chronic pain left me with little reason to examine what was going on inside me because my exterior world was interesting and rewarding.

But part of the acceptance – the change from ricocheting through life, blaming and complaining, to a more calm and thoughtful approach – came when I realized that as rewarding as my past life seemed at the time, a part of me was starved for something else – in my case, something creative.

I slowly came to the realization that my past life had robbed me of time to sit down with myself and talk. Yeah, I know that talking to the wall – *Shirley Valentine* style – sounds a bit bizarre, but it worked for me. To understand, I suggest you try this and see if it works for you…and don't tell anyone you're doing it. It's nobody's business but yours – part of taking ownership of your life. I found that self-talk worked best early in the morning when I had the house to myself and I was feeling reasonably rested.

This is the condensed version of my conversation with my wall. There's a reason I'm sharing this conversation, the one I've written about many times, in greater detail, in my journal.

And the reason is that listening to your inner thoughts and feelings about who you are creates the mental and emotional space needed for change.

So, here's a small example of me talking to the wall.

> **Me**: What am I going to do? This is so difficult, and I can't manage on my own. There's no one to help me, no one who understands what's happened. Even the doctors aren't able to help.
>
> **Wall**: What do you want help with?
>
> **Me**: Everything! Every part of my life has been tossed in the garbage by this damned pain! And nothing I try seems to work. The meds make me stupid. The pain never ends. I don't have a life! I don't know who the hell I am anymore!

Wall: Why do you think that is?

Me (to an obviously brain-dead wall): Because I've lost everything! Life is totally unfair. It's out of control and I hate it.

Wall: Well, what are you going to do?

Me: Me? What can I do?

Wall: (Silence)

Me: Why did this have to happen to me?

Wall: Why not you?

Me (Angrily): "Because I don't deserve it! There are so many things I wanted to do. I deserve a chance to be a hospital administrator. I've spent years getting a degree, an accounting designation and hours of learning to be a good manager. It was finally my turn to be recognized for what I was capable of doing.

Wall: Recognition? Is that all you want?

Me (after a pause): No, it's not all, but it's very important to me.

Wall: Who did you want the recognition from? Your family? Friends? You?

Me (thinking): I wanted recognition from…everyone…just this once.

Wall: Exactly.

I bare my soul and the wall gives me a one-word answer? Now I know why someone punches a wall! Thankful that no one was around to hear this, I pressed on.

Me: You mean that all my work was done for my own selfish reasons?

Wall: Partly, and it's good to have ambition and drive. But you also did it because you believe that this is how life is supposed to work. You are supposed to succeed, to be seen as successful. It's a part of who you are.

Me: Duh!

Wall: But success as you planned it is no longer possible. You cannot go back. There's no return policy on chronic pain. If recognition is what you're after, you'll have to find that somewhere else. So, who do you want to be now? What part of your life do you want to explore as you work on managing your pain? What opportunities do you think exist for someone in your condition?

I was about to yell, 'None, you stupid idiot! All the things I used to be able to do are denied me because I can't walk well. I don't have a day without pain. I can't—'

Then it dawned on me. **In order to get a life, I needed to take responsibility for creating change in my life and be open to the possibilities. I was the one left in charge of this sinking ship, and I could choose to salvage and repair it or abandon it – and by abandoning it I'd be abandoning my life.**

While I was railing away about the unfairness of it all, I failed to see that I was being offered the opportunity to dream about a life that incorporated my pain while it allowed me to pursue a different dream. Sure, this new dream was not the one I had planned or seriously considered before, because I believed in living the life I'd made for myself.

Trust me when I tell you that the journal pages that followed these self-talks were filled with 'Not possible,' 'I don't believe it,' 'Who made this foolishness up?' 'What's the point of trying if I'll only be disappointed when I fail?' 'I've had more than my share of disappointments; it's someone else's turn.' 'There's nothing I can do now, but learn to live with this pain until—'

Until what? There was the question.

Until I gave in to my pain and let it rule me? Until I drove everyone out of my life with my constant recitations of how I felt and what my pain was like today? Until I no longer liked or cared about who I was, or what might be possible in my new life?

Talk about a harsh reality!

But here's the deal. **Creating a dream of what your life could be like in the future, despite your pain, is your single most important act of acceptance.**

Acceptance doesn't happen all at once, sometimes it takes months or years. But I found something that helped the process – frequent periods of self-talk, such as talking to the wall, or you can write down your self-talk ideas. Writing things down often makes them seem more real, easier to understand and to deal with.

Try starting with this. Sit down with yourself and start with the ideas 'here's what I'm all about,' and 'here's what I want.' True, I probably can't have a life free of pain, but what's the best I can have? What are the new possibilities to choose from and work toward?

What if you accepted what you can't change at the moment, and moved on to make whatever accommodations you can for your pain? Would you then be more likely to find time to dream about your future?

For me, my first step back from teetering on the edge of giving up was when I realized that having to keep my legs elevated to ease the pain was not all bad. I had my laptop and I could easily sit in my recliner and work on my computer. What could I do on my laptop other than surf the net? I could turn my journal writing into a hobby…maybe even a career. Sure, first I'd have to learn to type. Then learning to write would have its challenges – good thing I'd already learned that problems often become opportunities if you have the right mindset.

Here's an important fact I'd like to pass on to you. People like us – people with chronic pain – have a clear advantage over those who don't. We're stronger and tougher than the average person because we've already survived loss and disappointment and are still willing to try again.

We have the two most important traits to bring about change in our lives – determination and resilience.

What is your dream? To work on regaining the mobility in your back and shoulders once you have the pain under control? To be able to go back to work part time or maybe full time when you feel better?

Whatever your dream is, make it happen. In the process of acceptance, you can begin the process of figuring out all the steps that must be taken to reach your goal, whether baby steps, or giant steps. Dare to dream of a life where you accept your pain, know how to listen to your body to minimize the pain potential and make the best of it as you begin your journey forward.

And here's another major consideration I discovered as I worked away to clarify all this for me – and now for you.

To make the most of your life with chronic pain, you must rekindle your passion for something that enriches your life.

You must return emotionally and spiritually to what you loved most in life before the arrival of pain.

Revisiting may mean you have to accept that certain activities in your life are no longer possible, but this does not mean you can't make a contribution to something else you're passionate about.

For instance, you may not be able to play ball, but you may find pain-free time to make calls or do paperwork or send out emails on behalf of the team. It may not be the activity you had intended to do, but changing your attitude and your mindset about what is possible will allow you to see your past life differently – not just in terms of what you've lost.

What I'm saying is that the new you, the person who is changing your attitude to your chronic pain, could develop your passion or interest in a different, even improved way. It may allow you to experience new and wonderful opportunities and offer chances for you to grow and learn in new areas you'd not considered before your chronic pain.

Believing and passion go hand in hand when it comes to acceptance of your chronic pain and moving forward into your new life.

One of the keys to acceptance is your belief in the power of you and what you're capable of when faced with adversity.

I remember in those early months that my belief in myself suffered a serious blow. My confidence nearly disappeared. I couldn't face the fact that this physically constraining gargoyle that turned my life into a one-episode-of-pain-after-another nightmare had invaded every corner of my life. Not only had I shut down my physical self, I had lost confidence in the idea that I could make my life work for me.

It was at this point that I had a moment of clarity about how the human spirit plays such a strong role in our lives.

Because we're busy humans we tend to ignore our spiritual side in the good times – even downplay its impact on our lives. We want to believe that who we are as human beings is mostly made up of what we've made of our lives, of what our present and our future hold – mostly by the possession of tangible items that showcase our role in this world.

It's only when things go awry, as is the case with chronic pain, that we are given the opportunity to look inward.

Why is it that when we feel we have nothing much left to lose, we find the will to keep going? And where does this willpower come from? I'm not certain, but my pain has taught me that when we are in need of it, we have an innate ability to overcome severe adversity.

To help you along with your acceptance of chronic pain, consider this. **Acceptance is a long-term shift in attitude and mindset, and it is up to you to begin the process as soon as you can.**

Here are a few practical suggestions I have discovered along my journey that might help you shift your mindset and begin the process of moving forward.

Don't wallow in the past – about how you ended up in pain, how you can't get rid of it, or what you might have done differently to avoid your pain. The past is just that – the past.

There is always the danger that you will over-think the situation as well. Thinking about your pain binds you to it and gives the pain the opportunity to run your life. On the other hand, if you get on with your life, despite your pain, you can redirect your energies toward other possibilities.

Realign your life to work with – not against – your pain. Pain forced you out of much of your old life, set you adrift to face a whole other lifestyle, and in the process it probably changed your view of the world and your role in it. But is that view of the world really helping you? Or might you be better off if you considered a new approach?

It's time to reclaim as much of your old life as you can. Or consider reinventing yourself – from a person who has chronic pain to this person who has the guts and determination to turn pain into a positive force in your life.

Make a list of life-affirming events you remember. Choose those moments where the preciousness of life was brought home to you, rather than those moments that were negative.

An example may be the moment when you found out you were going to be a parent, a grandparent, or the time someone you loved achieved a special milestone in his or her life.

Take those positive feelings of being part of life, or when you looked forward to something positive, and let yourself feel them all over again. Then hold onto each feeling, revisit that feeling every morning when you awake. Make those life-affirming feelings a permanent part of your daily life.

Start from this moment, and begin your new life with all its as yet unexplored possibilities.

Notes and Ideas

How would you describe your attitude at the moment? How has it changed since you started having pain?

How would you describe your outlook on life?

Do you feel that you've accepted that you have chronic pain?

If you don't believe you've accepted your pain, what would you like to change in your life to make it easier for you to accept your chronic pain?

If you were to try self-talk (talking to the wall or writing your self-talk in your journal), what would you like to talk about?

What change would you like to make in your life that would give you the greatest happiness?

5

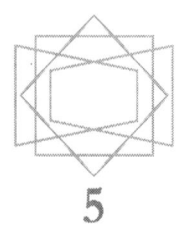

THE JOURNEY TO A NEW YOU – ACCOMMODATION

And now we come to what is probably the most critical part of learning to live with chronic pain. Emotionally and spiritually we need to work on learning to accept our pain, but while we're working on that, it is possible to rebuild our lives by making alterations to how we do things.

Often, we balk at the idea of changing our lives to accommodate our pain because we liked our life the way it was. It's not fair that we have to make all these changes! And we don't want to give pain that much power. Regret and wishing for the past create negative feelings, yet it's so easy to stay with these thoughts because over time, as we've mourned the loss of our past life, these thoughts become automatic.

Remember, negative thoughts are one of the biggest obstacles holding you back from your new life.

So let's talk about our mental attitude – our mindset. **If there is one part of us that we can control, and that needs to be nourished and protected, it is a positive mindset.** How we view our life in the presence of pain and our willingness to work toward a positive attitude is very important to how we accommodate our pain in our lives.

In the early months and years of my pain I wasted a lot of time wishing I could escape my pain so that I could go back to my old life. Because of this mindset, I came to believe that my fate was sealed – that all the effort on my part was for nothing and that my pain was in charge, not me.

One day when I was feeling down I began to see that my life had become one where I expected the worst to happen. I had become so pessimistic about my life that I no longer cared about how I looked, how I spent my time or what I did. I longed to go back to the past where I was in charge of my life. In the depth of this despondency, I had forgotten something important. **I was giving up on me – the person who I was certain deserved so much more.**

I also recognized that although I was gradually gaining control of my pain, I had let my pain dictate how I spent my days. I continued to focus on the next pain episode, its intensity, how long it would last and the restrictions on my physical abilities. There was a general sense by both my family and me that I'd been left out of life because of pre-occupation with my pain.

Remember, that for people with chronic pain and our loved ones – and friends who support us – learning to live around pain can be very time-consuming as well as emotionally and physically exhausting. Your life may lose its focus if you can't find a way to gain some control over the negative emotions of fear, sense of loss, problems with mobility, impact on family and pressing financial concerns, because these things leave you discouraged and increasingly unable to cope.

Out of this came a moment of realization. **I had abdicated the responsibility I had to myself and turned it over to my pain. I had let my life become something I didn't want, all because I was afraid that if I tried to accommodate my pain, I'd feel worse. That if I accepted my pain, I was somehow admitting that I had lost my old life, that I had failed.**

And I hate losing! But what sense did it make to get mired in this negative way of thinking about my pain?

Then came the moment when I realized that what I needed was some sense of moving forward, either with better control of my pain, improving my mental and emotional outlook, or both. I needed to feel I was making progress rather than being consumed by negative feelings.

The 'Things to Consider' list I'm about to offer may help you deal day-to-day with your chronic pain. As you read these suggestions, rewrite them to fit your special circumstances, or make a note in your journal about how you dealt with these issues and events in your life. Also, it's important to recognize that many of these actions will affect more than one area. They are interconnected, and working on one area will often provide relief in another area.

Pain Control is important. Do everything you can to develop a good relationship with your doctor so that the two of you can find the best possible pain relief medication for you. It's very important to not only get the right medication, but also to take the right amount, and that often takes time and a willingness by you and your doctor to be innovative. Your pain is as individual as your fingerprints, and only you can determine how much medication is necessary to give you a level of pain control you can live with. Expect trial and error in the beginning when it comes to getting the dosage right. And keep in mind that even after you've found a suitable level of pain control, something can happen in your life that changes how you react to your pain and the effectiveness of your medications, which could mean that you have to revisit the whole issue.

Pain medication is only part of the story in controlling pain. Along with pain medication, explore other avenues of treatment including relaxation techniques, acupuncture, acupressure, massage – and hold onto whatever works for you.

Start your journal and write…write…write. Every hour if needed. Get your feelings down on paper. By writing these feelings down, you take some of the emotional power from them, offering a measure of relief. Writing in your journal is like talking to a friend who simply listens and cares, with one advantage – if you don't want to expose your deepest feelings to anyone, you don't have to. Writing them down simply helps to ease the tension they cause. I discovered that my journal is not only a good place to write about my pain and the emotions around it, but it is also a good place to write about the good things that have happened….the joy you've brought to other peoples' lives despite your pain.

Over time, your journal will also show you what progress you've made in dealing with your thoughts around your pain. As you work on making positive changes in your life, your journal will reflect how these changes began to influence your approach to your pain.

I have some simple suggestions for you. I wish someone had shared these with me early into my life with chronic pain.

Learn everything you can about your type of pain. My clotting condition occurs once in hundreds of thousands of individuals – a fact that increased my feelings of isolation and fear. On the other hand, reading whatever I could find that was remotely related to my condition helped me feel in control, and subsequently I was able to have a more in-depth discussion with my doctor.

Take charge of your life one tiny step at a time. Start with the small things, like getting up an hour earlier to write in your journal, or doing personal care or setting aside time to do mild exercise. Something that I found very useful was to make a To Do List specific to my limited mobility with such things as going to the local pool, taking short walks or repotting a houseplant.

Taking time to be alone with yourself is essential. Find a quiet spot in the house and be alone with your thoughts. I discovered early on that with chronic pain I frequently needed to regroup mentally. I got the idea from my grandchildren who were learning about time out, which to them was a form of discipline. But time out in our case is when you take time to be with yourself and work on you and how well you're dealing with your pain. Call it positive time out.

Any-port-in-a-storm mentality. When we have a bad pain day, we need to do whatever we must to restore our sense of balance, to get back to being the person we really are. A bout of pain has a nasty way of reminding us just how vulnerable we are to its power. After I've had a day of unrelenting pain, I consciously choose something I like to do to give me back some level of control. After living hours without control, it is essential that I end the day – whatever time that is – with something I've chosen to do – listening to music, reading a book, or watching a TV program or a movie I love to watch. Sometimes the choice is simply sitting and talking with my husband about anything other than my pain. There have been days when I've had a glass of wine! I am well aware that wine and pain meds are a no, no, but the person who put that rule on the books obviously didn't live with chronic pain.

Remember you're not alone. At least one in five people lives with chronic pain. You and I and all those others deserve to be offered the respect we have earned for making the best of a bad situation. If you decide to reach out for support from other people with chronic pain, be sure they are doing positive things to help themselves and you live a better life with chronic pain. Choose carefully as there are groups involved with chronic pain who simply want a forum in which to air their complaints and negative issues around pain. You do not need to expose yourself to any unnecessary negativity.

Forget yesterday. Focus on today. Leave tomorrow for tomorrow. Fine advice you say, but how? I agree completely. I still have days when all I can think about is how miserable I felt the day before and dreading tomorrow's pain. But there are two things I consider when I get caught up worrying about how I'm going to make it through the hard days. First, I remember that I've been here before, and done this successfully for years. Next, I think about some aspect of my life that I like and can control. Sometimes I spend a couple of hours researching a subject on the Internet until the feeling of being trapped by my pain eases. One of the key ways to remain focused on 'today' is to keep my mind active.

Think about anything except your pain and its effects. When I need to refocus, I have a huge collection of books written about Jan Vermeer – my favorite painter – and I focus on reading about his artistic genius and let my worries about today, yesterday or tomorrow fade to the back of my mind.

And this leads to another very important point. It doesn't help to look at the long haul when you're having a bad session of pain because if you do, you will become depressed and discouraged and unable to do anything but wallow in self-pity about your situation. I also suggest you ignore all the stuff written about setting goals for managing your pain. What works for me is a very short-term goal that can be achieved in one or two hours. **In other words, take your day one hour at a time.**

Re-deploy your sense of humor. Sounds like I'm suggesting you move troops around, doesn't it? Not troops, but certainly mental resources and staying power. You need to make a concerted effort to see the funny side of things. Yeah, I know there's little to laugh about when you experience chronic pain. But...if you can find something funny each day, or if you can change something to make it funny, you will feel so much better. It will distract you from your pain and if you can laugh, the tension in your body that has been making your pain worse, will ease. Laughter truly is the best medicine. It is so uplifting and rejuvenating, and it improves your state of mind almost instantly.

My hint here is that if you are not able to see the funny side of an incident, rent a funny movie, one you know will make you laugh. One of my favorites is Planes, Trains and Automobiles. I've watched it dozens of times and still laugh. I can't think of Steve Martin without smiling.

Disappointment can have unpleasant side effects. One of the biggest hurdles in living with chronic pain is getting over disappointments. We have to face so many of them – from disappointment around our inability to find adequate pain control, or a sympathetic healthcare professional, to disappointment when we must face another day with no reserves of emotional energy left. Or we have to accept yet another change in plans because we don't feel well. And I know you can come up with hundreds of disappointing moments from your life with chronic pain.

Disappointment and discouragement have to be managed every bit as much as the pain does, and there is a reason why. If you don't come up with a way to deal with these two emotions, they can lead to depression – not because you're weak or 'crazy,' but because continuous, unrelenting bouts of disappointment will overwhelm the strongest person. I came to hate any form of disappointment because I'm the one who had to deal with it.

I discovered that the best way to deal with disappointment is to write my feelings down and then talk them out with someone who can offer support and guidance. When it involves your pain, it's easy to say why you're disappointed, but for other things, it may not be as easy to pinpoint the reason. Though difficult, it is essential that you sort out why you're feeling the way you are because negative emotions – like disappointment and discouragement – left to their own devices will dam up the feelings inside you, and your feelings will come out in other ways that won't be easy to fix. In the early months or years of your chronic pain, the person you talk to may be a family member or friend. As time goes along, it may be a counselor or psychologist.

I personally prefer a professional because, over time, your problems need someone who isn't emotionally invested in you. By that I mean you cannot expect those who care for you to remain impartial as they listen to your woes about the disappointments that occur in your life. Being there for you while you endure repeated disappointments over events in your life makes them feel useless. Because your loved ones are so deeply and emotionally invested in what you're going through, they are no longer the best people for you to share all your setbacks and disappointments with, especially when you're in the throes of recovering from a particularly difficult disappointment. You need someone objective and able to listen – someone who has the skills and experience to guide you as you work on your feelings of loss and disappointment.

The other big issue here is that if, despite your best efforts, you do suffer depression, the psychologist or counselor you're working with is in a position to recognize the change in your condition and suggest that you see your doctor concerning the use of anti-depressants. If, and it's a big 'if,' you do have trouble with depression, my suggestion is don't succumb to the lure of anti-depressants until you've experienced the results good counseling can offer you. Remember this – you're worth the best care available.

Say 'no' to time wasters. When your mobility is reduced because of your pain, it's very easy to spend hours watching TV, playing video games or surfing the net. On the other hand, if you reclaim some of those hours to concentrate on doing light exercise – tapping on a key board or a remote control doesn't count – or reading up on a subject you're interested in, you'll experience a sense of being involved, of having an opportunity to expand your life. I am well acquainted with the lure of TV and computer games, and initially wasted a lot of time on them – time that would have been better utilized by making changes in my life sooner than I did.

Keep Moving! Move around, move your limbs, stay in motion as much as your pain will allow. It's so easy to stay in the chair or bed or put off taking even a short walk, all because of pain. Yet mobility is important, not only to your general health but to your ability to cope with your pain. Look around you at the people experiencing pain, and you'll discover that almost all of them have lost some mobility because of their pain. Don't lose any more than you absolutely have to. Make mobility exercises a major part of your daily life. Being as active as possible not only improves your physical well being, it improves your mental outlook.

Don't Feel Guilty when you have a day or a few hours when your pain is easier to bear, or absent. Yes, this sounds crazy, but many people with chronic pain experience guilt when they have a day in which their pain is less. And you know why we feel that way?

Many people don't believe that someone with chronic pain really has pain unless they're demonstrating that they have pain all the time. The world at large has this weird urge to label us phony or they think we're some kind of charlatan if we dare to say or show that we're having a good day. And if we should dare to step up and enjoy life and are seen to be doing things others enjoy, then our audience might assume that during all those other hours, you and I were simply pretending to have pain.

I realize how cynical I sound here, and in all fairness, many people don't view our pain that way. But there are still those who take the position that if you have chronic pain, you are not permitted to have a pain-free day or days. For instance, when there's a sunny day after weeks of fog, wouldn't you be thankful for the sun and be eager to enjoy the outdoors? I'm sure those of you with chronic pain have experienced this phenomenon, and can relate.

But here's the important point, a theme of this book, if you like. **It's your pain to manage the best way you can. We know it comes and goes, but the key is that it always comes back. People who choose to think otherwise are not worthy of your time or your consideration.**

Don't let other people define who you are and what you do. I am referring to those who don't believe we 'really' have pain, that somehow we have an ulterior motive in claiming we do have pain – perhaps we are attention seeking? Or maybe we want to be excused from something. They may believe we don't really have that much pain – that we are exaggerating it. After all, they see us doing things that, in their estimation, a person with chronic pain shouldn't be able to do…as if they'd really know what we can and can't do. Stay away from these people. They're toxic!

Remember who's living with this pain… You are. Keep in mind that health professionals can offer insight into your pain, and offer treatment options, but they aren't living with pain. In the parlance of writing, they are supporting characters, supporting you through your pain. You are the main character, and most important of all, you're made up of so much more than just your pain. Show by your actions that you expect them to respect you as a human being and how you're meeting your challenge in dealing with your chronic pain. Become the manager of the team working on your pain, not a bystander.

Before I close this chapter and move on to how you manage the actual individual episodes of pain, I want to mention a few things that have been important issues for me. What I've learned might help you live a better life with your chronic pain.

Over time, I've come to realize that some people with chronic pain feel that unless they're in pain, day in and day out, they're not truly a person with chronic pain. I don't know if they take that position because they don't want to be labeled as having chronic pain, or they feel somehow inadequate sharing their experiences because their pain is generally under control and their lives are fairly normal.

Chronic pain is not about the amount or the intensity of the pain. It is about the fact that you continue to have pain. And despite your best efforts and those of your health care providers, you continue to experience some level of pain on a recurring basis.

When seeking the support of a health professional, find someone who inspires you to be the best you can be, not someone who tries to tell you what you should be. Life with pain is not about being lectured to. **It's about learning how to include your pain in your life, and about celebrating what you've accomplished despite your pain.**

And keep in mind there's no rule that says we must be perfect in how we accommodate our pain. We weren't perfect before the pain and we're not perfect now that we have pain.

But we are worth every effort we can make to be happy and content in our lives and we can integrate our pain into our lives.

Notes and Ideas

How would you change the 'Things to Consider' list suggested in this chapter? What would you add? What would you remove?

Do you feel you have a good relationship with your doctor? What would you change in your relationship with your doctor, and how would you go about it?

What treatments or therapies have you tried in addition to your pain medications? How successful have they been?

Are there any other treatments you'd like to try? If so, what are they, and do you know how to find sources for such treatments?

Have you considered keeping a journal about your life with chronic pain? If you did, what sorts of issues would you write about?

6
WHEN THE PAIN HITS…YOU CAN MANAGE IT

It's true. To a large extent, you can make your pain less.

So, let's start with what I consider two very common types of pain involved in chronic pain. The first is episodic pain that flares up. The second type of pain is one that is always there at some level of intensity and may include periods of increased pain. Needless to say each of these types has its own 'volume,' meaning the pain level can be severe, moderate or annoying but manageable.

Much of the time I have what I call 'housekeeping' pain. Any lifting, pushing, standing too long, sitting too long, sitting with my legs down – all these produce my housekeeping pain. It feels a whole lot like someone cut off the circulation to my legs as they begin to swell over my elastic stockings. Left unchecked, this pain will make its way up my body, getting worse as it continues. This usually can be relieved if I lie down with my legs elevated, and use an analgesic cream on the affected areas, or take a warm bath followed by the pain cream. This type of pain requires anywhere from an hour to two hours to go away. These episodes are painful and exhausting but after years of practice I usually recover from them fairly quickly.

But the pain that requires much more in the way of pain management is another sort of pain. I consider it to be what I experience during the acute episodes.

After twenty years I still cannot predict when this type of pain will happen, or what will bring it on. I do know that often before the pain begins, I experience a feeling of exhaustion so profound that I cannot function. I can best describe it as an aura or cloud that seems to surround me. When the pain gets underway it feels like a wave, moving from my abdomen down to my ankles, some of the pain is deep inside my body, the rest settles in my legs.

After some pretty awful bouts, I've found that what I'm about to offer here works best for me. A lot of what follows would seem automatic, but there are often other forces in our lives that influence how we manage our pain, which can result in our pain getting out of our control.

As soon as your pain begins, or starts to get worse, take your pain med. Don't hesitate, and be sure to take the amount that works for you. Find a comfortable spot, whether that be a bed, chair or whatever helps you to relax. If at all possible, find a spot with little or no noise.

Close your eyes and begin to breathe slowly and purposefully, while you 'listen' to your pain. Yeah, I know. Who's got the strength or the inclination to listen to something that hurts this much? But let me explain.

When I say, listen, I mean that while your eyes are closed, see if you can concentrate on the exact location of your pain. If, like me, your pain is so spread out there is no definitive 'one spot,' try choosing one from the many. While your eyes are still closed, let that pain be your entire focus. Ignore everything else going on, including anyone's expectations of you. Ignore everything but your pain while you concentrate on the area you've chosen. Calm your mind while repeating a phrase to yourself – a calming, positive thought that pleases you.

I've used the phrase, 'This will pass.' I've also found that quietly humming a soothing melody seems to set up a body rhythm that is helpful.

Try to imagine using a brush to color this area of pain, the tissues involved, while you imagine wrapping your arms gently around the area. Some people call this visualization and maybe it is, but what's important is that you concentrate on holding the pain area close in your mind. Somewhere in these next few moments, the pain med you took should start to kick in. You'll begin to notice a mildly warm flow of something that seems to make you feel...lighter. You all know how you feel as the pain med begins to take hold, so with your eyes still closed, continue to hold that pain area in your mind.

Or, while you're feeling the influence of your medication, begin to take deeper, gentle breaths and each time you breathe in imagine an aircraft controlled by your mind, one you've designed for just this purpose. Then direct your imaginary aircraft down your body ever so slowly to the pain site you've now isolated with your thoughts.

When you get the aircraft to the part of your body you're focusing on – still with your eyes closed – surround the pain area; cordon it off, if you will. Now, calmly focus every ounce of your energy – like a soft laser beam while you breathe out gently. Stay there, breathing slowly and try to relax every muscle near your pain area. You probably won't be able to do that the first few times. But I find that if I 'ride' the wave of pain medication flowing through my body as I concentrate on focusing on the pain area, the pain eases much faster and more completely.

If I'm having trouble relaxing, I picture my body lying completely limp in a bowl of Jello.

The key here is to be as comfortable as possible with little or nothing to distract you while you work with your pain medication to reduce the pain. Between you and your medication you can get your mind – your most powerful pain-control mechanism – and your body to work together to ease your pain.

Other times I give my pain a shape, such as a balloon. I imagined being able to shrink the balloon by surrounding it with positive thoughts and feelings, and as it became smaller I let go of any feeling or thought that made me tense. It was difficult at first, but every time I tried it became easier. Once I had a little experience in doing that, I could shrink the balloon simply by concentrating on uplifting thoughts and feelings.

Eventually I came up with two equations. Now I'm not a math student, but somehow the idea of an equation fit, and it made remembering the idea easier when I was in the midst of an episode of pain. Think about this:

Negative, aggressive, angry feelings and thoughts equal uncontrollable, persistent pain.

Positive, caring, nurturing thoughts lead to more controlled, less invasive pain.

One thing my long experience and many mistakes have taught me is that **anxiety, anger, fear and frustration are the perfect breeding grounds for pain.**

If you fight the pain, it fights right back. Negative emotions fuel the fight and make it much more difficult to control the pain.

Also, I discovered that when I'm stressed, fearful, or threatened with loss of control in another area of my life, it carries over to my pain. In fact, **any emotion that makes my body tense makes my pain worse or creates the perfect setting for yet another bout of pain.**

In order to ease your pain, you have to quiet these negative emotions, while letting calmer, happier feelings fill your heart and mind.

I've always had trouble dumping negative feelings. They seem to be so much more powerful than the positive ones. Believe me, it has taken a lot of practice to change my mindset from thinking negative thoughts to encouraging more positive, healing thoughts.

I still struggle at times to maintain a positive attitude. What I came to realize was that if I can change the underlying emotions, I can change how my pain behaves.

For instance, if at the beginning of a bout of pain, I let my negative thoughts and emotions – like fear and disappointment – take hold, my body tenses up, and I want to fight what's happening, rather than work with my body to ease the pain.

Your mind, along with your pain medication can reduce your pain, or at least make it easier to endure, and even a short reprieve may give you a chance to shut the pain down.

If shutting down the pain is possible, any technique is worth a try, isn't it?

Also, continue to write down your pain experiences so that you can see what works best for you. Then, if you can view what goes on with your pain in a positive, constructive light, rather than in a negative one, your attitude will prove instrumental in blocking the opportunity for negative emotions to rule you.

Another big advantage of writing about your pain is that, over time, your unique pain pattern will emerge. Finding this pattern is crucial and will help you determine what triggers your pain, what makes it worse or better and what works best to control it. When I reread my journal entries and discovered my pain pattern I found that if I could concentrate on breathing the negative feelings away I could ease the intensity of my pain, and shorten the length of time involved.

Sometimes the pain is worth it. This is another aspect of chronic pain, and it's one that often confuses those who live with us and care about us.

I'll give you an example of what I mean. Along with not being able to run or ski or jump, I can't dance without having a serious bout of pain. Yet, over the years, there have been moments when dancing with my husband at a party, feeling for a few minutes that I was part of the life so many people took for granted, led me to decide to dance. Why? Because sometimes the pain that follows is worth the chance to do something I love, regardless of how I will feel later.

I realize this doesn't make much sense to those people in my life who have seen me suffer with my chronic pain, or have had to postpone going somewhere with me because of my pain.

Deciding to dance, despite the potential for pain, still allows me to enjoy my life. Like someone who eats a huge Thanksgiving dinner knows it is going to result in raging indigestion, I choose to take part in certain activities I know will cause me pain. As in the case of the person who overeats, who wants the pleasure of lots of good food and good company, the person with chronic pain also wants the chance to be included in a special event. For me, dancing is special. For others it's gardening or some other physical activity that is generally denied them.

Besides, for just a few hours it feels good to be who you once were regardless of the resulting pain. You're entitled to feel good, to enjoy your life, and if that means you choose to do something that you know will result in pain in order to have a positive experience in your life, then go ahead. Remember, it's your life and your pain.

I just want to mention here that if you choose to do this, try to keep your pain episode as private as possible because those who care for you will find it hard to understand that you would do this to yourself. Remember that they are not you, and they can't truly understand, but you can show your caring and kindness by dealing with this episode of pain as quietly as possible.

In closing the chapter I'd like you to consider that one of the good things about dealing with recurring bouts of pain is that you have lots of opportunities to practice various techniques for controlling your pain, and you have all the time in the world to carry through and investigate all possibilities.

Take each episode of pain, and from it create an opportunity to try something different. As a kid taking piano lessons I used to loathe the phrase, 'practice makes perfect,' but in this case it's true.

I have one other point I'd like you to incorporate into your individual pain management plan. **That is that sooner or later you will find the right combination of pain med, relaxation techniques, activity, positive thoughts and feelings that give you an acceptable level of pain control. So hang in there, and keep trying.**

You're worth it.

Notes and Ideas

What types of techniques, other than meds, do you use to help with your pain?

The balloon idea is an attempt to visualize reaching out to the pain in an effort to control it. Do you have techniques that you've discovered that work? Why do you think they work?

Do you log your pain episodes and how they occur? Did you discover a pattern to your pain?

Does writing about your pain episodes help you to understand what is going on? Have you other suggestions on how to manage your pain?

Have you ever decided that the pain is worth it if you're able to do something you love? What was the response by those around you? Do you have further suggestions or ideas around this?

7

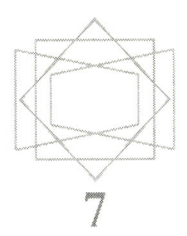

WHEN ALL ELSE FAILS – DARE TO DISCOVER

After years of trying to get my life back together, I finally felt as if things were going well. There were still moments when the pain would get the better of me, when I would wonder if the struggle was worth the effort, but I was content to cocoon myself in this tidy world of writing, maintaining my health and keeping my pain at bay. I was feeling more at peace than I had in years.

Then disaster struck. I suddenly started having more pain than usual, and began to feel that I was once again back in that place where pain ruled my life, where I felt powerless and alone. All my hard-earned experience was useless in the face of this new threat to my existence. I was headed back to where it all began. Pain, fear, anger and desperation left me wanting to swallow every pill in my arsenal of medications.

And my thoughts were anxious and self-destructive, leading to self doubt. Was I to blame for my pain? Was it something I'd done? What had gone wrong?

> ### Author's Note
>
> I need to digress here for a moment and talk about something I don't truly understand, but my experience suggests that it's true. When someone first has pain, it's acute, shocking and disruptive. Then for whatever reason the pain begins to 'put down tracks,' creates a sort of super highway between the pain sites and the brain.
>
> These tracks start out being the body's first line of defense in notifying the brain that something is badly amiss. But as time passes, these tracks continue to operate, self-fire if you will, as if on schedule. It is my belief that if you can stop the pain before the tracks get laid down, and the pathway becomes permanent, you can stop the advance into what I call the automatic stage – known as chronic pain. I have no scientific proof of this habitual misfiring of pain receptors, even without cause, only what twenty plus years spent dealing with pain has taught me.

If this idea of putting down tracks proved to be valid – meaning I'd feel routine pain even if a reason wasn't there – I owed it to myself to take every pain medication I could to allow myself to regroup and to prevent these new tracks for chronic pain from being laid. At least for the moment, whatever was causing this pain wasn't nearly as important as controlling it. What mattered was that I could not let this new pain become chronic. I knew I had to keep it in the acute phase…somehow.

One day during this new pain, I was taking my pain med when I realized something. I had never, in all the years I'd had chronic pain, taken the maximum dose of the pain meds ordered for a twenty-four period. I'd been trying to show how strong I was – and not be the kind of person to become addicted to pain meds. Often I would try to get by on less than half the morphine I was allowed in a day.

Determined, yet frightened, I took all the meds that were ordered over a twenty-four hour period, and promised myself that if I woke up in the night, with or without pain, I would take my pain meds. Then I worried that I might be making a mistake – that doing this wasn't really safe. I checked the med labels again to be sure I was following the directions and started my twenty-four hours of medications. I took every med prescribed for twenty-four hours, in the dosage and at the times allowed.

And guess what? The next morning my new pain had eased, and my old pain was quiet! What a surprise and what a wonderful feeling! Now, the pain did come back, but what's important here is that for a little while I was relatively pain free, and I was able to think in terms of what I'd accomplished and what that meant.

I vowed then and there, that should I require it in the future, I would take my pain meds around the clock for at least twenty-four hours, probably more. And I also promised myself that if the pain were not controlled by this regimen, I would convince my doctor to raise the dosage.

My life was back on track again, and I was armed with the knowledge that I had another tool with which to manage my pain. All was well in my life for several years after that until I had another pain develop in the same general area of my original pain. It was persistent and intense. I went to my doctor and had tests done to ascertain what might be causing the pain. I was forced back on regular doses of pain meds to control the pain, and meanwhile my life was on hold. Because of this new pain I couldn't sit anywhere. One doctor suggested that since I couldn't sit, I could lie down. There are no words to describe how I felt having received that so obvious, but unhelpful piece of advice.

But my biggest worry was that this acute pain could turn chronic in addition to my existing chronic pain. Frantic, I talked to my family doctor. She was helpful in ordering tests, but didn't really have an answer. Meanwhile, I fell into a veritable hole of self-pity and remorse.

I had no defense against what would likely transpire, given how hard I'd worked with the first pain. When I could no longer deny the reality that I was stuck in this space with this new pain, I demonized it, fought it, fought with it and I fought with anyone I had to deal with around it. Again, I wrote about it, and used every technique I could find to make it better. Nothing worked.

I've never come closer in my life to accepting that suicide was a way out of this. And as I said to my doctor, I have the tools to do it. I know I frightened him, and I scared myself, but I had nowhere else to go. I didn't know how to cope. I had used up all my other skills on the first pain, and I was out of options. No one understood what I had to deal with, and in my frightened mind, no one cared.

I believed I was truly and utterly alone. And that is not a dramatization. You had to be there to understand how it felt – for me a life with two chronic pains was unbearable. I had reached the end. I couldn't face another twenty years of even more pain that might never be resolved.

Desperate to control these frightening thoughts, I put every ounce of energy into trying to rework my situation. With the help of counseling those thoughts dissipated at least out of my day-to-day thoughts – but the need to find an answer became more powerful. With the help of my whole team, family, friends, and health professionals, I managed to get some control of this new pain, allowing me to focus on something I discovered by accident. For better or worse, chronic pain was part of the fabric of my being. It was as much a part of me as my eyes, legs, hands, my mind and all the other parts. Pain was part of me, of who I was, physically, emotionally and spiritually. So why didn't I see it as part of me, as deserving of acceptance as the other parts of me? Why wasn't I prepared to treat it with the same caring and respect as I treated any other part of me?

I had been fighting against an integral part of me. Whether I liked it or not, chronic pain was now a part of my physical makeup and I had to accept it as a permanent part. And where had the fight against an integral part of who I am gotten me? Not very far, was the answer.

Okay, so as I write this, it sounds a little crazy, but my new reality was even crazier. And if the best offering from the medical community was that I lie on my back, I knew I had to find my own way out of this mess.

I decided that when I had the next episode I would go somewhere quiet with my pain, and simply be there with it. I would respond with acceptance to the pain there, rather than with anxiety or fear.

When the pain started again I began treating it the way I would treat my tired eyes after hours at the computer. I didn't tense up and fight the pain. I simply took my pain meds, got into a comfortable position, and held the area with pain close in my heart and mind.

I've talked all along about accepting chronic pain in your life is a necessary step toward living well. But now I need you to understand the act of acceptance of your pain in a much more direct way. To gain a whole new level of pain control it is key that you accept each episode of pain as part of you, not as a foreign element to be beaten back, subdued or destroyed.

In order to accomplish this change to acceptance of each pain episode, and thus the pain itself, I let the pain, wherever it was in my body, into my consciousness. I was with the pain but instead of focusing on it, I focused on the part of me in pain – in a caring, nurturing way. I responded by giving caring attention rather than fighting the cause.

When I did this, each bout of pain became shorter and less intense. And I can honestly say that over the past months, I have had very little pain. When I do get it, I accept and care for the part of me that hurts, in the same way I would care for a child.

Through this process I discovered something critical to my emotional and physical wellbeing. **Unconditional acceptance of the actual physicality of the pain is essential to managing my life with chronic pain.**

I don't fight my pain the way I once did. I don't reject it, demonize it, complain about it, or call up any negative emotion. **Pain is no longer my enemy.** I accept that there will be opportunities to be with it.

Why does this approach work better than other approaches I tried? I think the biggest change is that I accepted that there would be pain in my life instead of treating pain as abnormal, as my enemy. I also began treating myself as a whole person, rather than compartmentalizing those areas with pain from those areas without pain.

After I changed the way I see my pain, I began to listen differently to others when they talked about their pain. What I learned was that each one saw their pain as a dreaded enemy, as if it were a war that had to be waged with an intractable foe. Their energy was focused on battle – not on nurturing themselves to help themselves. They expressed all the inherent fear, animosity, tension and negative feelings that such an approach produces. And how well I could identify with their approach! For years, fighting the pain seemed the only approach – much the same way we talk about fighting cancer – an approach that appears exhausting and self-defeating to me.

Thankfully I have left that approach behind. That's not to say there won't be moments and times when, for whatever reason, I won't cope as well as I'd like to, but that's okay. I have not lost a battle because I wasn't engaged in a war. I am at peace with my pain.

Many people will look upon this solution as a one-person remedy – one specific to my situation, but I don't believe that to be true at all. I am not exceptional, nor is my pain. I truly believe that pain needs to be accepted, that giving your pain the same level of acceptance and caring you give any other function in your body will offer you a new opportunity to control your pain. When you feel an emotion you don't deny it, because you know it is part of you. It's the same with chronic pain – it is part of you.

When you have pain, it's a part of your body that's in distress, and you're the only one in this universe of ours who can help ease your pain. Wouldn't you protect and care for any other function or part of your body if it were in difficulty?

I realize the idea that 'unconditional acceptance can ease pain' sounds way out there. And for skeptics or those afraid to consider that the mental, emotional and spiritual act of acceptance could have this kind of healing power, what I'm suggesting probably doesn't make sense.

But you see, for me there is a whole lot about chronic pain that doesn't make sense, starting with the idea that to date there is no cure for something that so many people have to learn to live with on a daily basis. That so much of what is offered as a treatment only treats the symptoms instead of the root cause.

My position is that those of us with chronic pain have to get by the best way we can and make our lives the best they can be. If that means trying something really different, then why not?

What have you got to lose by giving my idea a try?

Notes and Ideas

Do you feel you have adequate control of your pain?

If you don't, what would you like to see changed?

Are there issues related to your pain that you would like to discuss with your doctor that you haven't yet discussed?

Have you discovered new or different ways of dealing with your pain?

If you were to try my idea of unconditional acceptance of your pain, what thoughts or ideas would you need to change?

8

LESSONS LEARNED OVER TIME

For over twenty-two years chronic pain has been part of me, and it has heavily influenced how I approach my life. Living with chronic pain is a continuously evolving experience. If your pain follows my experience you will probably spend a lot of time and energy maintaining your general health and trying to control your pain. It is also very possible that as you get older, your pain will change – possibly for the worse.

To help with these realities, here are a few thoughts that might offer support.

Be patient and kind with yourself. The arrival of chronic pain in your life will alter how you think and feel. Give yourself permission to face the issues and problems that arise in your own unique way.

Believe in yourself and your inherent ability to find your new life with chronic pain.

Always be willing to **explore new ideas and techniques for controlling your pain.**

Put together a team of professionals to help you manage your pain, and trust them to offer you the best advice available.

Seek appropriate professional help whenever something changes, whether the change is physical or emotional.

Stay involved with your family and friends.

After twenty-plus years of working away at this whole conundrum of how to manage chronic pain, I believe the next couple of considerations are key to finding your new life after the arrival of your chronic pain.

The first of these is **find purpose in your life.** And again, it sounds so simple. Everyone should have a purpose in life, but it's even more important for the person with chronic pain. As you work on managing your chronic pain, having a purpose becomes a key to living successfully with pain. Searching your heart and finding your purpose will offer you a healthy focus – an alternative to worrying about and exacerbating your pain.

I like to think of purpose as passion in action. And believe me this passion for something outside yourself will see you through the darkest moments of your pain.

Whether you find purpose in the spiritual realm, or you find purpose helping those less fortunate or simply in loving your family, what matters is that you are giving of yourself to something or someone outside yourself. Those positive feelings will reward and nurture you.

The second is **being your own best friend, and taking care of yourself will reinforce your belief in yourself, and confirm that your life with chronic pain is truly worthwhile.**

As I said before, one of the side effects of chronic pain – if it is not controlled – is that pain shuts you down, makes you turn in on yourself. You lose interest in others and life around you. You get so involved in dealing with the grinding every-day-of-every-year aspects of your pain that you forget that you're a whole lot more than just someone living with pain. Involving yourself in an outside interest draws you out of your pain and allows you to contribute something special to the rest of the world.

It is important to remember that before you developed chronic pain, you had skills that provided you with a pleasant life. **These skills may be altered now, but the underlying ability to enjoy what you love hasn't disappeared.**

The third issue is to **conquer the 'victim' mentality.**

One of the most self-destructive problems you will face is feeling victimized by your pain and the healthcare system. These feelings of being a victim, of being treated unfairly or not being understood, are toxic to your physical and emotional health.

Having said that, I realize that in so many ways, we can't help but feel like victims. At first we are at the mercy of our pain, our changed circumstances, and a healthcare system that doesn't understand how powerless we feel with pain as a part of our everyday lives. Many times the system that is supposed to offer hope and support turns us away when they can't find an acceptable solution. Yes, at times we have been victims of the world around us, and the anger and resentment created in us by this victimization can be overwhelming. Feeling like a victim comes with a whole array of other feelings like anger, fear, impatience, disappointment and discouragement – to mention a few.

Try working through the problems that make you feel like a victim. Concentrate on each one you've identified and see if you can change even a part of it by some sort of action. Think of it this way: You and your problem aren't going anywhere soon, which means you've got lots of time to work on finding ways to improve your life.

The bonus? When you feel less like a victim, you pass that lighter feeling on to those around you. They respond by seeing you in a more positive light. Their changed attitude makes you feel more accepted by them, more part of the community you live in together.

The fourth issue that we all face is how to deal with failure. As people with chronic pain we face our share of failures, beginning with the failure to regain our old life and retain our old image of ourselves. Feeling that you've failed can linger for a long time, adding to the sense of despondency that can accompany chronic pain.

On the other hand, **failure is part of life, regardless of whether we have chronic pain or not.** The only people who don't experience failure are those people who refuse to try, who avoid any kind of risk. Yet in the end, they may experience the worst kind of failure in a failed life.

Our feelings of failure come from a mistaken belief that because we've failed to get our old life back our lives have lost meaning. We allow ourselves to believe that after months and years of trying to accommodate and accept what's going on, we are no closer to finding a life around our pain than we ever were. But I found a way out, and that's the single most important thought in this book. **There is a way to take back your life despite your chronic pain.**

You need to develop a personal philosophy that allows you to get past this sense of failure.

Let me explain something that helped me. After my first fiction book was published, I had a party. A lifelong friend of mine – who is also a fabulous cook and homemaker – made three celebration cakes for the party. They were lovely, delicious and a big hit with everyone. But what I will always remember about those cakes was the message she wrote in colored icing on them. **'Life is not about waiting for the storm to pass, it's about learning to dance in the rain.'**

Reading those words was a critical moment of enlightenment for me. Chronic pain is the rain in my life. I can either learn to dance in it, or I can withdraw, admit defeat, become a victim of my circumstances and hope that the pain will pass. It won't. It never will.

My fifth issue is this that over the years, I felt compelled to take the advice offered and set goals because goals somehow demonstrated that I could deal with my pain. I suggest you **try not to set yourself up for failure by setting too many goals or by setting goals you can't achieve in one step.** Anyone with chronic pain realizes early in their pain that multiple goals meant to be carried out simultaneously often leads to failure on at least several of them. And failure is one of the biggest enemies of a person with chronic pain who is trying to improve their life. Pick one goal you feel you have a reasonable chance of meeting, and aim for that. One small success at a time is the real goal.

The sixth issue is education because learning about techniques for controlling chronic pain is important. I would suggest you read as much as you can on any subject you feel might offer you relief. It's important to stay informed about new developments in the treatment of chronic pain. There are over five hundred books on the Barnes and Noble website dealing with aspects of chronic pain.

Because there is so much out there on different types of pain, and on different treatments, be sure before you go and empty the shelves that the book or material you're reading will specifically address the issues you have around your chronic pain.

On many occasions, I've started to read a book or article only to discover that the author is talking more about acute pain than chronic pain, and, as I clarified in this book, the two are distinctly different conditions. In my mind, acute pain and chronic pain are about as similar as a sailboat and a submarine. The only thing they have in common is that they both need water to get around. So it is with chronic and acute pain, all they have in common is that they can occur in the same person at the same time.

Chronic pain is a multi-system disease that affects the entire body for months or years, while acute pain is isolated to one area and lasts only for a few days or weeks.

Another point when selecting reading material is that many books deal with a specific aspect of pain, a specific treatment or therapy that may or may not be applicable to your situation. If you think that one of these treatments or therapies might work for you, I suggest you discuss it with your doctor before you try it.

The seventh issue is one of pain management. **Pain medications are only a partial solution.** If you are to succeed over the years, you need to see yourself as more than someone with chronic pain, but rather someone who is a complex individual dealing with a disease that affects your entire being. As I said earlier, your solution to putting pain in its place in your life will involve a combination of many different techniques, ones as individual as you are.

And finally, my eighth issue – **Watch out for the pitfall of feeling inadequate.** There are so many opportunities for you to feel inadequate! So often it feels as if everything we attempt to do to manage our lives only goes to prove how inadequate we are at finding solutions – from pain management to mobility and lifestyle issues.

When reading some of the material out there, or listening to a health professional, I found myself constantly feeling that I was inadequate because so much of what was suggested seemed so simple. What was wrong with me that I couldn't follow their easy instructions?

As I rooted around the bookstore shelves looking for the answer that would make me feel better, I discovered that the authors of books on chronic pain didn't know any more about it than I did – less as a matter of fact. But because they had certain credentials behind their name, I thought they knew more than I did.

Don't let this happen to you. Judge what they are saying against what you know to be true in your life. And remember, what they know may be book-orientated, not life-orientated.

In closing, please remember that your chronic pain is about you, about rebuilding your life, and it's about understanding who you are, what you need, and how you cope.

Treat yourself to all the time and the emotional space you need to look after yourself.

Respect your need for mobility, rest, diet or other physical issues that are key to making your life the best it can be, with as much physical freedom as possible.

Celebrate the uniqueness of who you are and what you've accomplished.

Celebrate your strength and courage in living everyday with pain as part of your life.

By accepting, integrating and coping with your disease, you will have given yourself the ultimate gift.

You will have reconstructed your life, changed your understanding of what chronic pain is, and chosen to live successfully.

My wish for you is that one day, you too can dance in the rain.

About the Author

Ruth Stella MacLean is a retired registered nurse with a Bachelor of Commerce Degree from Mount Allison University. She is a retired Certified Management Accountant and obtained the designation of Canadian Heath Service Executive before leaving her position as Director of Ambulatory Care at the Moncton Hospital in Moncton N.B. Canada. Among her responsibilities as Director of Ambulatory Care, was the management of a Pain Clinic that dealt with treatment of chronic pain.

Ruth Stella MacLean writes from the unique perspective of a person with chronic pain as well as a nurse and hospital manager for over fifteen years. She understands the medical system and how it works. This knowledge helped her manage her pain but did not go far enough in assuring her complete rehabilitation from a life of pain to a life of fulfillment and happiness. Living Successfully With Chronic Pain has real solutions offered by someone who has lived life not only as a healthcare professional managing a pain clinic, but also as a person who has received the best care the medical profession has to offer people with chronic pain.

Yet it was not enough. This shortfall between what the medical model has to offer, and what the individual with chronic pain needs, is the focus of this book.

She maintains a website for those interested in issues around chronic pain. www.livingsuccessfullywithchronicpain.com

During her professional life as a hospital director, and later as published author, Ruth Stella MacLean gave speeches, workshops, radio and newspaper interviews, and continues to do speaking engagements and workshops whenever the opportunity arises.

She's a published fiction author under her pseudonym, Stella MacLean. She is presently under contract for two more Super Romance Books to be published by Harlequin. If you'd like to know more about her career as a fiction author, please visit; www.stellamaclean.com

OTHER WORKS BY RUTH MACLEAN

HEART OF MY HEART

BABY IN HER ARMS

A CHILD CHANGES EVERYTHING

Ruth can be reached at
www.livingsuccessfullywithchronicpain.com

Twitter: @Stella__MacLean

Facebook: https://www.facebook.com/profile.php?id=100001166463953

CPSIA information can be obtained at www.ICGtesting.com
Printed in the USA
LVOW082108150413

329247LV00001B/363/P

9 780987 829504